A Little Book of
HEALING MAGIC

D. J. Conway

THE CROSSING PRESS

The Crossing Press
www.crossingpress.com

A division of Ten Speed Press
P.O. Box 7123
Berkeley, California 94707
www.tenspeed.com

Cover design by Victoria May and Chloe Nelson
Cover art by Rafael Lopez
Interior illustrations by Petra Serafim

Library of Congress Cataloging-in-Publication Data is on file with the publisher

ISBN 1-58091-146-3

First printing, 2002
Printed in the United States of America

1 2 3 4 5 6 7 8 9 10—05 04 03 02

Contents

CHAPTER ONE

What Is Healing Magic?

Healing magic. These two words describe a method of using spiritual connection, physical means, and magical spells to heal the body, mind, and spirit, not only of humans, but also of animals. For tens of thousands of years, this method was the only technique used. And it was used successfully. Then "modern" medicine took over and decreed that only physicians trained in a certain way could heal and that the spiritual and magic did nothing. This viewpoint still exists.

Originally, the word magic, which may come from the word *magi*, described the learning that was taught to the priests and the sages of the Medes and Persians. These healers were famed for their skill in working enchantments, which also included incantations, divinations, and astrology.

Many people get upset whenever the word magic is mentioned. However, magic is only supernatural until science and explains it. An example is alchemy, which was a skill practiced in secret until chemistry was validated. Astrology was the foundation upon which astronomy was built. The use of magic wouldn't continue if it didn't get results, even if we don't understand exactly how it works.

However, today people are beginning to question this attitude. According to a number of recent surveys (not by physicians or hospitals), more than 60 percent of people believe in using alternative medicine, prayer, and/or magic along with orthodox medicine. Whenever the general populace questions enough about methods of healing, accepted techniques begin to change. Fortunately, more doctors and medical centers are becoming open to alternative healing methods.

The connection between healing and magic was a valid and successful concept from the beginning of the human race. The separation began when the healers of later cultures condemned magic as an invalid practice and separated it from healing.

The original definition of *magic* was not the same as the corrupted meaning attached to the word today. Don't bother to look up the word in any dictionary, as they only give the meaning attached to stage magicians. The true meaning of *magic* is to draw universal, spiritual energy from the Otherworld, mold it by concentrated thought into a specific desire, and release that energy-thought into this world to manifest.

This definition applies to strong prayer as well as to magical spells.

Many people who apply healing prayers to illnesses call the positive results miracles. Miracles have nothing to do with scientific reason or what a person supposedly does or doesn't deserve. This places miraculous events in the same category as the results that magic produces. In magic, the healer should never question whether the recipient is worthy of healing, but work on the belief that all humans are worthy of healing. The condition of each person's soul and what they do or don't deserve is between each individual and the Goddess/God. Miracles, whether by prayer or magic, don't have to make sense to us or the scientific world. If they did, they wouldn't be miracles.

You do not need to be a shaman to practice the healing in this book, nor do you have to be knowledgeable about magic or psychic healing. This book is for laypeople who are concerned about a loved one's illness or perhaps their own illnesses, and desire alternative ways to work for healing.

Although the ideas and practices of alternative healing in connection with magic discussed in this book can be used by anyone at any time, they are meant to be used along with orthodox medicine, not to supplant it. I do not recommend that you stop orthodox treatment for any disease. And as a healer yourself, you should never recommend that any person stop orthodox treatment or medication in favor of something you think is better. Erroneous recommendations lead to legal problems.

Although this book does not address herbal medicine, I feel a word of warning on their use is needed. If you delve into the use of herbs for healing, be certain that you understand exactly how they will interact with any orthodox medicine before taking them. And never assume that the healing will be faster if you take more than the recommended amount of herbs. Herbal medicine acts slowly, so be patient.

Also take extreme care that you know the toxicity of certain herbs, regardless of what some books advise. For example, I know of one book on cancer that recommends toxic quantities of wormwood. Herbal medicine is an exact science and is best understood and practiced only if you train in the field or have the benefit of a person certified in herbal medicine.

This book is not slanted toward any one religious group or idea. Goddess/God is known by hundreds of different names that all strive to define an unknowable force in the universe. There is no difference between the prayers to saints and the prayers to ancient deities. The same energy is attached to burning a candle at church as to burning a candle at home. The only difference may lie in the amount of concentration, determination, and desire put out by the healer and the patient.

For any healing to take place, healing magic requires total cooperation between the healer and the patient. The patient must take an active part. In other words, the patient must be responsible for their illness and do everything they can to facilitate the healing. Otherwise, the healing will not be permanent, if it occurs at all.

You should be aware that some patients, consciously or subconsciously, do not want to be healed. Some patients like the attention they get from their illness or the control they can exert over family members and friends because they are sick. No matter what you do, you will not be able to heal these people. All the time, effort, and energy you pour into trying to heal such a person will be wasted.

The same applies to the roles of family and friends in healing. If there is a persistent negative, pessimistic, or hateful attitude or atmosphere around a patient, it can harm instead of heal. At the very least negative attitudes can interfere with healing. If this type of attitude exists in only one person, or in a small number of family and friends, the patient is best advised to sever communications with these people. However, that must be the patient's decision. This action will be of little use if the patient does not have other positive-minded friends and family left, unless the patient has a strong will and is willing to form new friendships. Positive support systems are vitally important to getting well.

Sometimes you will encounter a patient with a serious illness who truly wants to be healed, but the process doesn't seem to work no matter what you do. In these cases, it may be that the patient's lifespan is at its end. The patient may not consciously know this, but their subconscious does. When this happens, work for peace, spiritual harmony, and freedom from pain and fear.

Some of the methods presented in this book may not seem magical at first, but they are. Remember, all magic requires that you draw upon universal energy for healing, that you mold it into a specific desire in your mind, and then release it to manifest in the here and now. It doesn't matter if the magical process is prayer or spells, for the same rules apply to all magical healing. The same rules apply whether you are a healer working on another person or a patient working on yourself.

You do not need to use all the methods mentioned here, but I do ask that you read the book in its entirety before choosing a method with which you feel comfortable. You may use any of the methods in any combination. In fact, using more than one method seems to raise more healing energy.

The practices in this book may also be used by the patient, either with or without a healer. The best healer is you, anyway. No healing, even if aided by the most proficient of psychic healers, will occur unless the patient cooperates and takes an active part.

CHAPTER TWO

A History of Healing Magic

Healers have been in demand from the beginning of humankind, for accidents and illnesses of the body, mind, and spirit have always been with us. These early spiritual healers were shamans; shamanism is the world's oldest spiritual healing profession. The traceable roots of shamanism date from the Stone Age, at least forty thousand years. However, common sense tells us that the profession of shamanism must go back even further, before humans felt any need to record their activities in cave paintings.

Although the descriptive word used to designate a shaman was different from culture to culture, the training and practices of a shaman were remarkably similar everywhere in the world, even today. In this book, the word *shaman* is used to simplify the description, although the word *shaman* comes only from the Tunguso-Manchurian dialect and means "to know."

People generally connect shamanism with the Eskimo, African, and Native American cultures. However, a branch called Celtic shamanism existed for centuries, finally dying out in Scotland and Ireland as the cultures succumbed to the power of implanted religions.

Out of necessity, the early shamans (both men and women) were a combination of healer, magician, and priest. Early peoples knew that healing, magic, and the spiritual were inexplicably intertwined and should not be separated. The primary purposes of shamans were, and still are, to travel to the Otherworld in their spiritual bodies, to work positive magic, and to mediate and communicate with spirits and deities in the Otherworld. In this way they are able to retrieve information that is unknown on the ordinary levels of consciousness. This especially applied to healing of the body, mind, and spirit. Shamans needed their spiritual abilities (altered state of consciousness) to contact the Otherworld to determine the cause of any illness and what herbs or practices were necessary to treat the disease.

When tribes or clans became too large for the shaman to do all the work alone, this responsibility was frequently divided into two separate categories: priest-magician and healer. However, people in both categories were instructed in the same practices. For example, although healers focused on the healing arts, they also understood that a strong connection with spirit or the Otherworld and the magical energy of that world were necessary for any healing to take place.

Throughout history, cultures continued to have their priest-healers who were required to know magic themselves or work closely with those who did. The ancient cultures of Sumer, Babylonia, Ur, and Egypt had groups of priests, healers, and magicians who were trained in certain temples and expected to work together. We know this because of the surviving clay tablets and papyri. Even the ancient Greeks had their shamanistic equivalents, particularly those who worked in the sacred *asklepieia*, or temples of the healing god Aesculapius. The patients in these Greek temples were treated by physical methods, magically induced dream therapy, and communication with Aesculapius.

This treatment of the whole person by spiritual connection, physical methods, and magical spells continued in the Middle East and Mediterranean areas until the end of the fifth century B.C.E., when Hippocrates of Cos appeared. His admonitions that only the body was involved in physical illness and that spiritual and magical techniques were unnecessary and useless challenged the ancient premise that body, mind, and spirit were vitally connected. He declared that only physical methods could cure illness, an unfortunate attitude that has persisted in today's medicine. He did mention healing hands, but he did not mean healing with the hands. His limited definition of healing is still taught by every Western medical school.

Fortunately, many of the alternative healing practices of the Eastern cultures have survived and are in sharp contrast to Western medicine. In Western medicine, only dysfunction and disease are treated. Eastern healing treats the whole person. Western medicine views the patient as only a body. Eastern medicine views the patient as an inseparable combination of body, mind, and spirit, all of which interact constantly. This Eastern idea is known as holistic health.

In ancient China, the physician was paid only as long as the patient stayed healthy. As soon as the patient became sick, the payments stopped. Thus, physicians were motivated to help people heal quickly and keep them well. In Western medicine, some physicians view healing in terms of how many treatments and how much money they will receive for their services. Common sense will tell you that the ancient principles and ideas behind Eastern holistic medicine are more valuable to healing than those of a traditional Western physician. Unfortunately, Western ideas have corrupted some of the orthodox Eastern physicians. However, many of the ancient ideas of alternative healing practices behind Eastern healing have been kept alive and are still practiced.

We are fortunate today that the old knowledge of magical healing is being reclaimed and presented to the reading public. The old methods have been refined and modernized to fit our present society and needs, a process that is vital in all healing methods. This makes it possible for anyone to combine magical healing with orthodox treatment.

If your religious background makes you uncomfortable with certain healing methods in this book, skip them or convert them into an acceptable practice. Magic isn't static and is open to change. The magic doesn't occur because a certain spell is done in an exact manner, although doing such a spell will help you concentrate the healing energy. The magic lies in your finding a way to an altered state of consciousness in which you can mold universal energy and manifest it in this physical world.

The healing profession looks as if it may be coming full circle, and that is good. Sick people should be able to use every method at their disposal to get well again.

CHAPTER THREE

The Aura and the Chakras

Before you can effectively use any healing technique, you need to understand a few ancient and basic ideas. These ideas will help you work better, be more confident in what you are doing, and concentrate the healing energies in the correct places, which will make a huge difference in whether your healing efforts don't work, work a little, or work well.

Energy creates everything in the cosmos. Einstein's theory of relativity and his formula, $E = MC^2$, is based on that concept. However, Einstein was only rediscovering a very ancient truth known to many cultures. This universal, spiritual energy was called *mana* by the Polynesians, *prana* by the Hindus, and *ch'i* by the Chinese. Because everything is composed of energy, then everything, without exception, can be affected and influenced by energy. This definitely includes deliberately directed energy, whether positive or negative. This is the foundation of truth behind the workings of magic, which is the directing of energy for a specific purpose and the affecting of an idea, object, event, or person by this energy.

Every living body, whether human or animal, is surrounded by what is called an aura. Many cultures also believe that every object, whether animate or inanimate, has an aura, which is why we speak of a crystal or an area in nature as having vibrations.

The aura we will study here is the human aura. This aura consists of layers of various types of energy that surround the physical body. The aura's energy is affected by the universal energy that is everywhere in the cosmos. These layers are also affected by the energy molded by individual thought and action. The aura can be powerfully affected when that energy is gathered and directed by will power.

The aura is a kind of electromagnetic field, and can be compared to the field that surrounds the earth. We can't ordinarily see the earth's electromagnetic field, but scientists know it exists because of gravity, the air it traps around the planet, and the way it makes a compass point to the north. This electromagnetic field around the earth gets denser as one moves closer to the planet from space. Without this field or atmosphere, the earth would have no life and would not be a living entity itself.

The same applies to the human aura. We are surrounded by an electromagnetic atmosphere, which allows us to exist.

When this atmosphere becomes fatally contaminated or destroyed, the body dies. The inner layers of the aura, the ones closest to the physical body, are denser than the outer layers. This denseness also makes the inner layers of the aura easier to detect with the hands or a pendulum.

Many scientists have studied the existence of the aura within the last one hundred years or so. Mesmer called it magnetism, Jussieu the electric fluid, Reichenbach the odylic flames, de Rochas the exteriorized sensibility, and Dr. Baraduc the vital rays. The only two scientists, however, to discover a way to show the aura in scientific experiments were Dr. Walter Kilner and Dr. Semyon Kirlian.

Just after the turn of the twentieth century, Dr. Kilner, a British physician and not a psychic, created chemical dye screens using dicyanin dyes. These screens revealed the human aura to untrained eyes. He used these screens to diagnose various physical illnesses and mental conditions. He was extremely accurate and in 1911 wrote a book on the subject, *The Human Atmosphere*. This book is still in print under the title *The Aura*. Because what he learned was so unorthodox, Dr. Kilner was attacked by the medical profession and the hospital where he worked, and his medical license was revoked.

A weak version of his invention is found today in aura glasses. Actually, these glasses are nothing more than dark violet plastic held in a cardboard frame. You can get the same results with a piece of dark violet photographic lens plastic held over your eyes. The color helps to open the Third Eye or brow chakra and makes you more sensitive to seeing the aura. Aura glasses are fun to use but don't become dependent on them.

You can train yourself to see at least the two inner layers of the aura by using a simple technique. Stand in front of a mirror in a darkened bathroom. The only light should come from a half-open door or a dim nightlight. If you wear glasses or contact lenses, remove them; in this case, perfect sight is not beneficial. Look at yourself in the mirror. Focus your gaze slightly beyond your image and let your eyes go out of focus. You may find that squinting your eyes slightly will help. Take your time and don't try too hard. In a moment or so you will see a thin light around your body. This is your aura. In some cases, you may also see what appears to be another face overlaying your face. If this happens, you are seeing yourself in a past life.

If you have people to work with, you can use another technique. Have one person stand a few feet away from a blank dark wall or in the doorway to a darkened room. Place either a small candle at a safe distance behind them, or have a dim nightlight there. Everyone else should stand about four to eight feet away from this person, viewing their form against the dark background. Use the same eye instructions given above. Take turns looking at each other. In this way, you can see the differences in people's auras.

In 1939 a Russian couple, Valentina and Semyon Kirlian, developed high-frequency photography that revealed the aura on film. The Russians called this bioplasmic energy. Although Kirlian photography can record on film the state of health, mental conditions through means of energy moving around the body, and whether the emotions present at the time were positive or negative, the scientific world outside of Russia refused to accept this physical proof.

The most recent aura energy researcher is a Japanese physician named Hiroshi Motoyama. He has developed an electronic instrument that can measure the effect of acupuncture and chart the meridian lines in the body. The meridians are rivers of energy that run along specific pathways in the physical body. His findings have elicited little interest in the scientific community outside of Japan.

Knowing about the aura, universal energy and how it affects the aura, and how to use this energy to heal the aura is a vitally important part of magical healing. If the inner layers of the aura are sick, the physical body will have disease. If the outer layers have problems, it is possible to prevent this trouble from moving closer and affecting the body. All disease works from the outer layers of the aura inward, until it manifests in the physical form.

Some people are born able to see the auras of others, while most others can train themselves to see it. And with just a little training anyone can feel the aura. We all feel it subconsciously and react to certain people getting too close to us. This reaction occurs because a person's aura may not feel comfortable when it comes in contact with ours.

As a beginner, don't have unrealistic expectations of what you will see or how it will feel when working with the aura. If you have expectations of some flashy or really spectacular occurrence, you will be disappointed. Most psychics don't receive flashy impressions. Good psychics never gush on about violent colors, reciprocating movements (whatever that is), or dissociate harmonics. They are more likely to feel hot, cold, prickly, or a flare of energy within an aura. Some don't ever see colors but see only light. Some don't see either of these, but flashes of colors or symbols in their mind. Remember, your experiences will likely be different from those of other aura readers and workers, so don't judge yourself by them. Also, your experiences may change as you practice aura healing and become more comfortable with it.

I have found that the aura itself is composed of nine layers. Not all writers will agree with me about the composition of

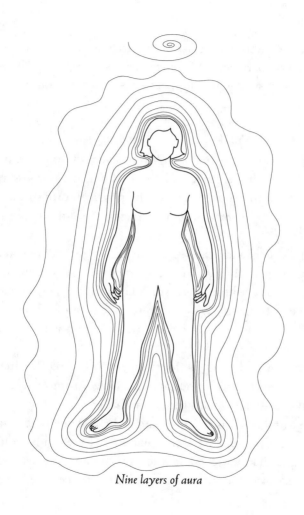

Nine layers of aura

these layers, their numbers, or what they reflect. I base my information on personal experience. The best way to learn about the aura is to start with simple exercises to find your own energy field.

THE NINE LAYERS

The etheric body, the first aura layer, is very close to the physical body, sometimes only a matter of a half-inch or less away from it. It reinforces the shape of the physical form so that the soul or spirit will be contained. It corresponds to the root chakra.

The physical aura, the second layer, is tightly connected to the first layer. This layer reflects exactly what is going on in the body at any time and is associated with the belly chakra.

The emotional body is the third layer. Our emotions and our feelings shape this layer and it corresponds to the solar plexus chakra.

The mental body is the fourth layer. It is directly affected and impacted by our thoughts and how strongly we think them. It is associated with the heart chakra.

The astral body is the fifth layer, the essence that links us to the astral plane. The astral plane is where many guiding spirits, guardian angels, and ancestral beings live, as well as where deceased people continue their existence. We travel in the astral body when we sleep at night, when we do shamanic journeys, sometimes during deep meditations, or whenever we have a near-death experience. This layer is associated with the throat chakra. The first five layers of the aura are the ones most commonly seen with the physical eyes.

The sixth layer links us to parallel universes, other dimensions, and cross-time travel. It is also deeply linked to psychic phenomena. It is associated with the brow chakra.

The seventh layer is associated with the past, present, and future. It will often hold clues to past life experiences that are influencing the present life. It is associated with the seventh, or crown chakra. However, layers six through nine are difficult to find and read, particularly for healers without a lot of experience.

The eighth layer is an iridescent egg-shaped layer that can extend as much as four feet beyond the physical body and often has waves of energy rippling through it. This layer reflects the spiritual growth and connection, or lack of it, in the patient. It is connected with the eighth, or transpersonal chakra, that lies above the head.

The ninth layer, sometimes called the ketheric layer, is the only layer that does not completely surround the physical body. Instead, it exists as a small whirling vortex above all the other layers. Because it is associated with the ninth chakra, or universal chakra, it connects all the other layers with the world and energies of spirit.

As a beginner, do not expect to detect all the layers. It is uncommon for healers to feel more than the first three or four layers until they have practiced for a very long time.

The first exercise is simple. Work in a positive, relaxed atmosphere where you won't feel self-conscious about what you are doing. Rub your hands briskly together for a few seconds. Then hold your hands, palms facing. You will feel a warm, tingling ball of invisible energy between the palms. Slowly move your hands away from each other until you feel the tingling and warmth begin to dissipate. Move your hands back toward each other until you can feel the sensation again. You have just felt the extent of your own aura between your hands.

Practice this exercise until you are comfortable doing it. You will discover that the extent of your aura will change according to your physical condition and mental attitude. If you are tired or depressed, the aura draws in upon itself and appears to become smaller. When you are elated and feeling refreshed, the aura will expand.

Many healers will rub their hands together just before working on a healing. This sensitizes the minor chakra centers in the palms of the hands and makes them open up for the

Energy flowing between hands

drawing in and giving out of universal energy. This action will also make the hands more sensitive to the aura of the person on whom they are working.

The next exercise requires a partner. If you don't have a human partner, you can work with a pet. Rub your hands briskly together as before. Then, keeping your hands about two to four inches from the partner's body, move your hands up and down and around their body. You will feel the same warm, tingling feeling emanating from them. This is their aura. You are feeling the dense inner layers of the electromagnetic field that surrounds them.

If you discover a place that seems hotter or colder than the rest of the aura, you have discovered a possible trouble spot. You can pour universal energy into this spot by holding your hand there and visualizing white light pouring into it. Visualization requires that you trust your instincts to make the connection with universal energy and pour it freely through your own aura and body into the patient. Without visualizing, you will pour personal energy into the patient, not universal energy. This will cause you to leave yourself depleted and possibly vulnerable to illnesses. If done properly, you should feel exhilarated because of the influx of universal energy, some of which will remain within your own aura.

If the patient is extremely ill, you may not be able to pour in universal energy fast enough. In this case, it is possible for the patient to drain off your own aura's energy as well. This psychic draining happened to me when my husband was unconscious with cancer. He was drawing off energy faster than I could channel it. I allowed it to happen so he could be healed, but most people may not be able to stand the exhaustion that follows. I chose to put myself in a precarious position because I was determined that he would not die. Many healers cannot stand up under such an onslaught, so think carefully before you allow this to happen.

Unfortunately, you may also experience this psychic draining from people who are not ill. Sometimes they are referred to as the psychic vampires because they feed on the energies of other people. Most people guilty of this don't realize on a conscious level what they are doing. They can be the friends who show up feeling depressed and miserable but who leave full of energy. Then you feel depressed and tired. The only way to defend yourself from such people is to throw up a blue psychic shield around you and hope for the best. Or avoid these vampires entirely. To construct a psychic shield, visualize yourself surrounded by brilliant blue light, or see yourself wearing shining blue armor. Pour more energy into this shield if you feel it weakening.

If you are a novice at aura healing, or if you don't feel comfortable with the draining that can happen during a healing, break the connection at once. Immediately wash your hands or at least wipe them several times against your legs or sides to make certain the connection is broken. This is a good method to practice whenever you have completed an aura healing, as it makes certain the auras' ties are broken.

Sometimes, you will discover what is known as a flare in an aura. In this case, the field abnormally jumps out from the person's aura in a long flare. These flares are usually caused by emotional distress of some kind. Left unattended, they can burn a hole in the aura's layers and let in diseases. Touching a flare may bring with it mental images or feelings of the emotion that caused the problem. If you suddenly feel anger, sadness, or depression in a flare, that is a good indication that the patient is either going through or just passed through intense events that triggered such feelings.

Again, try to seal the hole with universal energy. You may have to smooth over this flare several times before it will stay in its proper place. However, unless the emotional distress is remedied, the flare will soon pop out in the aura again. As in all healings, the patient must actively take a part in their own healing and be responsible enough to correct what needs correcting on a physical level.

Every time you touch an aura in healing, even for a brief moment, you may make a significant change, so be certain you are in a positive frame of mind. Otherwise, you may transfer negative energy even though you don't mean to. Always finish an aura reading or healing by swiftly moving your hands from the top to the bottom of the aura, thus sealing it again.

You need to practice touching auras as much as you can with a variety of people. For this reason, it is nice to work with a group of people studying aura healing. In this way you can acquaint yourself with different auras and broaden your own understanding of the subject. Also, you will notice that an aura will change from one time to the next, depending upon what health or life conditions the person is experiencing.

CHAKRAS

The aura is closely connected with what are called chakras. *Chakra* is a Hindu word that means "wheel of fire." Traditionally, there are seven major chakras, although there are many minor chakras also. The chakras are whirling vortexes of energy in the aura and etheric body that suck in universal energy when they are working properly. If partially or completely blocked, a chakra will cause a breakdown in physical, mental, emotional, or spiritual health. This results in illness.

In Hindu belief, the Prana, which is universe energy, comes in seven colors that match the seven major chakras of the human body. These colored universal rays constantly move into and out of well-balanced chakras, keeping the body healthy and vital. If you want to do complete magical healing, you need to acquaint yourself with these chakras, where they are, what they do, and learn how to put them into balance.

There are eleven important chakras of the etheric body, and a gemstone is associated with each chakra. Some writers believe there are thirty-two major and minor chakras, but these eleven are the most important in healing.

The chakras radiate out from the spinal column to the front of the body and connect with the etheric body, or that portion of the aura that is closest to the physical body. Healthy chakra colors are pure, not dark or muddy. Impure colors signal a disease or possible problem. The size, shape, and intensity of the colors reveal the development and health of each person. Partially

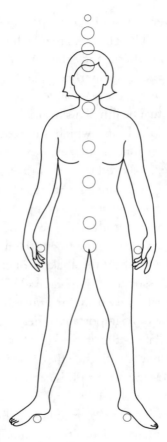

The chakras

blocked chakras are common, because we live in an imperfect physical world and are not perfect beings.

As with the aura, not all healers will see the chakras. However, they can be felt with the hands and imbalances will respond to a pendulum. Sometimes the chakras will create a feeling of color or condition in your mind. Learn to trust your instincts when working with the chakras for healing. Your first impression will likely be correct.

Never work on just one chakra, particularly the root chakra. Overstimulating one chakra will cause major imbalance in all of them. You can do major harm by working on a single chakra. Instead, work on all seven major chakras during a healing, beginning with the root chakra and working up to the crown chakra.

You will notice in reading the descriptions of the chakras that diseases can be related to more than one chakra. This happens because the chakras are all connected.

The first chakra is the root chakra. This is found at the base of the spinal column. The traditional color is red, and the associated glands are the ovaries and testes. This is the survival center and corresponds to physical needs and survival instincts, procreative urges, will power, and the establishment of success or failure. Imbalance in this chakra can cause circulation problems, depression, infertility because of slow ovulation rates or low sperm count, low energy, irritable bowel syndrome, colitis, spastic colon, Crohn's disease, chronic constipation, adrenal dysfunction, Addison's disease, depression, chronic fatigue, allergies, anxiety, premature aging, anemia, frostbite, neuralgia, paralysis, or troubles with the menses. Stone: garnet.

The second chakra is the belly chakra, sometimes known as the spleen chakra. It lies just below the navel in the center of the abdomen. Its color is orange and the associated glands are the adrenal glands that lie atop each kidney. This chakra is vital because it transforms lower energy into higher. Blockage is common because many diseases occur from mental or emotional patterns of thought or emotional traumas. Work on this chakra for many types of nervousness, eczema, difficult skin diseases, coughs, exhaustion, menstrual cramps, arthritis, sexual disorders, the kidneys, worry, defensiveness, hatred, menopausal problems, mood changes, hormonal decline, urological problems, impotence, prostate and testicular problems, trouble with the lower back, and uterine, cervical, and other general sex organ difficulties. Stone: carnelian.

The solar plexus chakra lies just above the navel in the center of the abdomen. Its traditional color is yellow; it is associated with the islands of Langerhans located on the pancreas. These glands regulate the amount of insulin released into the body. Clear this chakra when working on stomach and duodenal ulcers, diabetes, insomnia, flu, fear, exhaustion, indigestion, constipation, irritable bowel syndrome, malabsorption syndrome, hepatitis, gallbladder trouble, cirrhosis of the liver, pancreatitis, diabetes, swelling of the spleen, all types of abdominal cancers, emotional frustration, deep emotional pain, bitterness, and deep fear. Stone: tiger's eye.

These three lower chakras are the most earthy and are connected with earthly emotions and needs as well as energies. The next four upper chakras are more closely connected with a mixture of earthly and spiritual energies.

The heart chakra is located in the center of the upper chest. Its color is green, and the associated gland is the thymus. Unblock this chakra when working on diseases of the heart and lungs, high blood pressure, coronary artery disease, arteriosclerosis, asthma, chronic obstructive lung disease, the stomach, intestinal trouble and ulcers, the eyes, sunburn, headaches, infections, difficulty with the blood and bones (particularly with cancer in these areas), repressed emotional pain, insecurity, deep loneliness or love loss, autoimmune disorders such as lupus, rheumatoid arthritis, and polymyositis. Stone: green or watermelon tourmaline or rose quartz.

The throat chakra is in the front area of the throat just above the points of the collarbone. Its color is electric blue or turquoise and it is associated with the thyroid glands. Use healing on this chakra for pain, burns, sleep, calming of emotions, headaches, inflammations, infections, swellings, fever, menstrual cramps, laryngitis, colds, flu, tonsillitis, mastoiditis, poor thyroid function, chronic laryngitis, parathyroid gland lesions, esophageal cancer, laryngeal cancer, and irritations of the throat, sinuses, and the nose. Stone: lapis lazuli.

The brow chakra is located in the center of the forehead, between and just above the eyes. This is also the area of the psychic Third Eye. Its color is indigo or a bluish purple; its gland is the pineal. Clear this chakra for headaches, muscle spasms in the neck and shoulders, deafness, mental and nervous disorders, pneumonia, eye and nose disease, hypothyroidism, hyperthyroidism, anxiety, depression, insomnia, Alzheimer's disease, migraines, strokes, multiple sclerosis, chronic pain, and lingering negativity of thought. Stone: purple fluorite.

The crown chakra is located at the top of the head. Its gland is the pituitary, and its color is violet or white. Rarely you will see gold in this chakra. Spiritual awakening in this area will connect the person to the eighth and ninth chakras, which are associated with realms of high spiritual growth. Unblock this chakra for stress, sleep problems, stress diseases, nervousness, low melatonin secretion, low immunity, diseases of the physical brain, spiritual imbalances, cataracts, mental disorders, and tumors and diseases of the scalp, skull, and brain. Stone: amethyst.

The eighth chakra is the transpersonal chakra, which lies about eighteen inches above the crown of the head and is not directly connected with the physical body. It is a transitional chakra that mediates between the physical and the spiritual. Its color is pure white or a flashing of rainbow colors, as seen in a crystal when exposed to sunlight. No physical diseases are directly associated with this chakra. However, on rare occasions you may see a deep spiritual disease here, one that has lingered or continued through several lifetimes. Stone: clear quartz crystal.

The ninth chakra, or universal chakra, lies about six inches above the transpersonal chakra. This chakra is totally disconnected from the physical and has only connections with the pure spiritual part of a human. It is a direct pipeline for each person with the Goddess/God or Supreme Universal Force. No diseases are ever found in this chakra, although it may be almost completely closed due to lack of spiritual growth. Stone: clear quartz crystal or rutilated crystal.

The eighth and ninth chakras rarely need to be worked on during a healing, as their energies and purposes are so esoteric that it is difficult for a healer to manage them. The patient, however, can clear these with prayer and meditation.

The minor chakras in the palm of each hand are very sensitive; they can send out universal energy, as well as gather and direct it toward a physical person or a mental goal. It is frequently helpful during a healing for the patient to hold a crystal in each hand.

The other minor chakras in the sole of each foot are useful for drawing earth energy upward into a patient. Because we are beings of the earth, we use a lot of earth energy as well as universal, spiritual energy. This earth energy helps us maintain our connection with the planet earth and deal with everyday life. These chakras are also important in that they allow us to discharge negative energy back into the earth where it is transformed into positive energy. They also ground us and siphon off excess energy. It is beneficial for people to walk barefoot whenever possible for these reasons.

See the appendix for the chart on chakra stones.

There are three methods for working on the chakras, all of them simple to learn and use. In the first, the patient lies on their back in a comfortable position. Now simply lay the appropriate stones over the areas for each chakra. Put the stone for the crown chakra leaning against the top of the head. Place a clear quartz crystal in each hand and near the sole of each foot, with a larger clear quartz crystal just above the crown chakra stone. Beginning at the root chakra and ending with the universal chakra, hold your dominant or power hand over each stone as you tone "Om." If you can't bring yourself to tone "Om," instead say "Amen." When you finish, sweep your hand from the universal chakra down to the root chakra. This draws down high spiritual energy to flood each chakra and break loose any obstructions.

The second method requires the use of a pendulum and one-inch squares of correctly colored paper to match each chakra. Lens plastic is especially good and can be purchased at photography stores. Again, you work from red (root chakra) to violet (crown chakra). Before beginning this pendulum-chakra work, determine which is your power hand. Ordinarily, the power hand is the one you use most of the time. However, in a few individuals, they may find that the power hand is the opposite of the one they use. Go with the hand you feel most comfortable using.

If you are working on yourself, hold the pendulum in your power hand and an appropriately colored square in the palm of the other hand. Hold the pendulum over the paper while you visualize the chakra on which you will be working. If there is a blockage, and thus a decreased amount of energy in

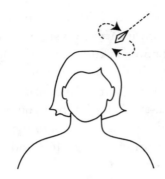

Using a pendulum for the aura and chakras

that chakra, the pendulum will circle clockwise or counterclockwise until the correction is made. If the chakra doesn't need work, the pendulum will not swing. When finished with one chakra, take up the next colored square in order, and repeat the process. Continue to do this until you have treated all the chakras.

If you are working on a patient, have them lie on the back in a comfortable position. Hold the pendulum in your power hand and the appropriately colored paper square in the other. Hold the pendulum over the patient's corresponding chakra and visualize the color. Again, the pendulum will swing clockwise or counterclockwise until the correction is complete. Continue up to the seventh chakra at the crown of the head.

Some pendulum users disagree about the counterclockwise swing. However, this assumes that all people react in the same manner when detecting chakra energy. Pendulum swings and energy detection differ from person to person. With practice, you can determine which is the correct swing for you when using a pendulum. When using a pendulum for chakra correction, there doesn't appear to be a specific reason why the pendulum swings one way or the other. For most healers, a clockwise swing will be normal.

The third method of chakra cleansing again requires the patient to lie on their back. Hold the palm of your power hand above the area of the root chakra and your other palm above the area of the second chakra. Tone "Om" or "Amen." Move the power hand to the second chakra and your other hand to the third chakra, and tone again. Repeat this process, moving up one chakra each time until you reach the crown chakra. While you hold your power hand above the crown chakra, hold your other hand above the root chakra. This links all the chakras and causes energy to run in a continuous loop through these light centers.

Chakra and aura healing are simple magical healing methods. They are easy to use and very effective.

CHAPTER FOUR

The Healing Touch

For thousands of years many ancient peoples were healed by touch and magic. In the temples at Malta and Gozo, the sick slept in huge stone chambers, while priestesses there communed with the gods and did their healing magic. Egyptian healing books dating as far back as 1,800 B.C.E. combined healing and spells. In the early Irish Celtic society, healers at a royal hospital, called the *Bearg*, or House of Sorrows, at Tara used special magical stones, water from sacred wells, charms, and magic, as well as herbs and surgery. The Irish medical schools were so highly esteemed that students came from all parts of Europe to learn the techniques. All ancient healers were connected with the spiritual in some manner.

Ancient Oriental healing methods describe meridians and nadis (pronounced naw-dees) running through the body. There are twelve major channels for the ch'i, or universal energy, to flow through, with many other branching channels.

These all end in the fingers and toes. Think of meridians as rivers, streams, and tributaries for universal energy that flow in specific channels and do not change. They are all connected to nerve endings in the physical and etheric bodies. Both the meridians and chakras take in cosmic energy and distribute it to every body organ. The aura holds this energy in place unless the aura is damaged.

The Chinese use these meridians or streams of energy during acupuncture treatments. If there is a blockage in the meridian, the acupuncture treatments release it. Some of these meridians are also used in reflexology and acupressure for the same results. If you decide to use any of the points known in acupressure or reflexology, take great care when working on the very young, the elderly, or the very sick. Sudden breakage of blocks of negative energy can overload the body and the aura, thus making the patient even sicker. In Japanese shiatsu massage, the therapist uses both acupressure and a special kind of massage to break blockages in the meridians.

I do not recommend using acupressure or reflexology unless you study these subjects in depth. It is too easy to think you know all about acupressure and reflexology after reading a book, but both subjects require training to be used correctly and successfully.

Healers must have some spiritual path in their lives, even if it is only the belief in a supreme creative force, a power without a name. Having a spiritual path is not the same as belonging to a church or group. Technically you don't have to believe in a superior force to heal, but I've yet to see a nonbeliever be able to accept the fact of spiritual healing. The healer and the patient need not believe in the same spiritual path to create a healing. It is not the healer's place, either, to discuss religion with any patient.

Healing by touch involves not only the accepted tradition of laying on of hands, but also aura massage, aura cleaning, and aura sealing. It requires patience, dedication, and practice to learn. You don't have to be psychic, nor do you have to practice a certain religion. As long as you have a spiritually motivated desire to help someone who is ill, you can get results.

Before you begin, you must decide which is your power hand and which is your removal hand. Ordinarily, your power hand is the one you use most often. If you are right-handed, this would be your right hand, and your left hand would be the removal hand. If you are left-handed, it would be the reverse. Hereafter, when the power hand is mentioned, you should use the hand you determined was your power hand.

The power hand draws in universal energy and directs it to the aura or body when healing someone. The removal hand

The power hand and the removal hand,
with energy flowing in and out of these hands

draws off negative or excess aura energy and returns it to the earth or the cosmos, where it is automatically recycled into positive energy. In other words, you put in with your power hand and take out with your removal hand.

Before undertaking any healing methods on a patient, you should first systematically check the patient's aura and chakras with your hands. Check and rebalance the chakras with your pendulum, (see chapter 3). Then run your hands through the outer layers of the aura. Look for hot or cold spots, places that seem to leak energy, hard and inflexible areas, and the long flares that shoot out from the aura. A badly diseased site may make your hands feel burned or frozen because of the intensity of the blockage or the violent release of energy.

A person may be able to hide their true character when interacting with others, but it always shows in the aura. The aura will always reflect a person's habits, tendencies, emotional moods, and physical condition, as well as any potential or existing diseases.

Until you have practiced for many years and become proficient in handling cosmic energy, I do not recommend touching a patient's body during a healing. Until you learn how to regulate the flow of energy through your hands, touching patients' bodies may transfer the energy too quickly and cause greater disruption of their aura. Keep your hands two to four inches away from the body at all times.

Also remember that everything in the universe, even a single thought, is composed of energy. Therefore, wherever you place your attention, the cosmic energy you pull into your hands will follow your thoughts to that place. This is especially important to know when working with the aura, for you must direct the universal energy both with your hands and your thoughts.

There are five main aura disturbances that may cause health problems: 1) slow leaks, lesions, and tears; 2) more toxic or negative energy than the aura can process; 3) flares; 4) stagnation of energy in any one place; 5) collapse of aura areas. All of these disturbances must be healed and sealed before the patient can recover.

Slow leaks and tears will emit small seepages of energy. These will feel like moving tingles on the palm of your power hand. They are usually caused by minor emotional difficulties or life problems. People may have many of these little tears during the course of a day, and most of them seal themselves. However, if a person is dealing with a major problem or an attitude that may attract a disease, these unhealed leaks and tears can allow greater damage to occur.

A lesion feels like a small rough spot in the aura. It is the site of a past damage that didn't make it completely through the aura's layers. This is like a scar on the physical body and is a potential area for future problems unless softened and sealed by cosmic energy.

A flare can be caused by two things: too much unprocessed energy in an aura or a huge disastrous break in an aura. Having too much energy is similar to hyperventilation. The aura and chakras become clogged with excess energy brought in by the subconscious during a time of stress. This energy will churn purposelessly until it sours and changes into negative energy. In this case, a flare is an aura's attempt to rid itself of this "infection." To correct this, the healer must use their removal hand to help draw out the negative energy. Then using the power hand, the healer must seal the break. This type of flare will feel either very cold or very hot.

The flare caused by a huge break may feel like energy rushing out, rather like a hole in a dam. The patient will likely feel extremely tired all the time. Such flares are always caused by large emotional traumas or extremely serious diseases. You should begin by massaging and cleaning the aura, as explained later in this chapter. Then balance the chakras. Follow this by holding the power hand over the flare for some time and doing the usual aura smoothing.

Stagnation of energy in one place will create hot or cold spots in the aura. This can be either a site for an undetected disease or a potential one.

A collapsed aura is usually found in patients who are extremely ill or close to death. You may also find a collapsed aura in someone contemplating suicide. A collapse can manifest in two ways: 1) the aura is so close to the body that it appears to be almost nonexistent; or 2) the aura has deep indentations. The indentations will feel like large inward dips in the patient's aura, as if a chunk of aura has been removed. The deeper the pit, the more aura layers are involved. This indicates a disease that has reached the spiritual levels or that began there. In cases of collapse, the healer must work on the seventh and eighth aura layers first, because no input of cosmic energy or chakra rebalancing will hold until these levels are repaired.

Disease or illness is primarily a disruption and imbalance of a body's chakras and aura. Negative energy works its way inward through the aura's layers until it affects the chakras and meridian lines in the etheric body, thus causing blockages. Blockages are congested pools of negative energy that break down the physical body's resistance and often provide food for bacteria and viruses or mental or spiritual collapse. This condition creates openings and opportunities for a disease to manifest itself in the physical body. Because all disease is considered an imbalance, it is possible that epidemics may be caused by imbalances in an entire group of people.

It is extremely difficult, if not impossible, to detect exactly what caused a disease. To cure a disease is impossible without full cooperation of the patient. Diseases can arise for a number of different reasons. Past or present emotional traumas and constant stress, which weaken the aura, may be to blame. So may severe and persistent character flaws, such as extreme, constant impatience, revengeful attitudes, compulsive behavior, or constantly dwelling on the negative. Other culprits can be an inherited family tendency or a past life tendency toward a specific disease. A healer can heal the visible physical symptoms by repairing the aura and rebalancing the chakras. However, unless the patient does much introspection and makes conscious changes in spiritual outlook, lifestyle, habits, and diet, the healing will not hold.

Other accidents and diseases may have more of a physical cause, such as man-made substances like chemicals. In the case of accidents, something in the lifestyle or life path plan weakened a portion of the aura, which then allowed the accident to happen. Man-made substances may weaken the aura and then damage the physical body. Everything works from the outer layers of the aura inward to the physical body.

Instead of searching for the root problem or passing judgment, you should concentrate on healing the aura and chakras. If you receive mental pictures of symbols or inwardly hear a message about a cause of disease, you must determine if the patient is open to these before passing along the impressions or messages. It is a patient's responsibility to make changes that will aid the healing. Always suggest ways for patients to self-heal, never demand that they do it. And *always* ask patients if they wish to be healed before you begin.

When you prepare for a healing, have the patient sit in a straight chair or lie on their back. I prefer the chair method, because the patient does not have to turn over during the healing and the healer can move easily around the patient to check all sections of the aura.

Before you begin a healing, and between healings of more than one patient, you should always calm your mind by taking several slow, deep breaths and saying a prayer. In fact, it is very beneficial if the healer takes time to meditate briefly before doing a healing.

Visualize yourself surrounded by a brilliant white light, as if the sun were directly over your head and shining straight into your crown chakra. Feel any negative energy in your body and aura pouring out through your feet into the earth. When the negative energy flow ceases, feel the earth energy flow up through your feet and mingle with the sun energy. This visualization connects you to both the spiritual cosmic energy and the grounding earth energy of this planet.

Those who are ill can also use this exercise to help heal themselves. Drawing in the white fire of the sun also helps treat cancer, while the softer, gentler earth energy is useful for soothing all illnesses.

Next, briskly rub your hands together. Then cup them about six to eight inches apart so you feel the energy ball between them. If your energy isn't strong enough, do more deep breathing and repeat the sun fire visualization. Then rub your hands again to check your energy. A weak healer always runs the risk of inadvertently drawing off energy instead of putting it into the patient's aura. A weak healer can also pick up disease symptoms from a patient.

To begin an aura massage, balance the patient's chakras, (see chapter 3). This will move the blocked energy of the chakras either out of the etheric body entirely or deposit it into the aura, as in a difficult case of illness. To remove this transferred negative energy or any previously residing negative energy from the aura, you need to break it up by massage and scrape it away.

For the best results in aura massage, you need to work through the aura in a definite pattern. Begin in the aura around the head. With your power hand, work the aura with your fingers in a downward scratching motion. Work over the head and down the neck first. Use the side of your removal hand to rake or brush the aura in a downward movement. This scrapes the negative residue off the massaged portion. Flick your removal hand frequently when doing this. Continue the massage and raking motions over the left shoulder and down the left arm to the fingertips. When you reach the fingers, scrape the residue off the hand with a flicking movement of your removal hand. Go back to the right shoulder and repeat this massaging and scraping until the right arm is cleared. Do the same over the back and chest to the waist, then massage and rake over

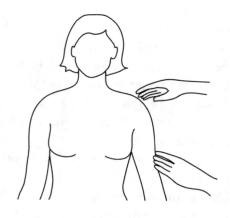

Raking off negative energy

each leg to the feet. Always flick off the residue when you reach the fingers and toes.

When massaging and cleaning the aura in this manner, you may discover hard or resistant spots. This area can feel like a callous or a hard scab. Negative energy has been in this area so long it has solidified and will take extra work, perhaps even extra healing sessions before you can break it loose.

After washing your hands or rubbing them briskly against your legs, go back and smooth the entire aura from head to feet. Check for any flares, tears, or leaks in the aura that you may have missed in the initial work. If you find any, seal them by creating balls of energy between your hands and applying this directly to the troubled area with your power hand. Hold the energy there with your hand until it attaches. If the problem area is a flare, remember to pull out the excess energy with your removal hand before attaching the energy ball. Until you get the excess energy under control, you will not be able to successfully seal the aura.

Repeat the chakra balancing with your pendulum and then seal the entire aura again. Ground the patient by placing your power hand in the outer aura layers while you visualize all excess energy flowing into the earth through your removal hand.

While some believe a healer can't pick up negative energy from a patient's aura I have found that this transfer of negative energy is possible, particularly if the healer's body or mind has problems that resonate with the patient's. If you suddenly find yourself dealing with anger, sadness, depression, or vindictiveness after giving a healing, you probably picked up negative vibrations from the patient. In this case, quickly run your hands through your aura from the head to the feet and wipe away these energies while they are still on the outer layers.

Try not to do too many healings in a day or a week. You can become too tired if you stretch your efforts and time too much. A properly done healing requires more time than a beginner would think. Only healers who have practiced for many years should do more than one or two healings per day.

If you have no healer to work on you, you can do the aura massage and cleaning by yourself. However, it is more difficult to find trouble areas in your own aura.

CHAPTER FIVE

Meditation and Visualization

Meditation is a vital part of healing for the physical, emotional, mental, and spiritual bodies. Unfortunately, many people still think of meditation as sitting in a full lotus pose with a blank mind. Unless you are adept at yoga, you will have to force your body into the full lotus pose, and all you will be able to think about is pain. Fortunately, this isn't the only way to meditate. In Western meditation methods, it doesn't even require that you keep a blank mind.

Meditation is simply a method that helps quiet scattered and racing thoughts. By doing this, it reduces stress and heals the body, mind, and spirit.

Meditation in its many versions has been around for centuries, and is part of many religions in one form or another. The word *meditation* is derived from the Indian Sanskrit word *medha*, which means "doing the wisdom." It can also be traced back to the Latin root word *meditari*, which means "to muse or ponder."

Most religions recognize some form of meditation, whether it is simply prayer and contemplation or saying a rosary. Using prayer beads during a meditation is an Eastern—and Western—practice. But meditation can be practiced by anyone of any religion or anyone without a religion. It is a method to calm your emotional and physical bodies and relieve stress. Since 50 to 80 percent of all illnesses are stress-related in some manner, meditation is a valuable tool for healing.

Caregivers are frequently forgotten partners in treating a sick person. The stress on a caregiver increases dramatically when the illness is extremely serious or long-term. This stress increases if the caregiver has no one to help. This places the caregiver at risk for illness. Meditation is an inexpensive therapy the caregiver can practice without leaving home.

Scientists have discovered that meditation has a direct beneficial effect on the physical body. It can lower blood pressure, control pain, speed healing time, calm heart palpitations, lower body temperature, relax the breathing, and help build the immune system. Meditation calms, relaxes, and can even make you drowsy by raising serotonin levels. Serotonin is a natural brain chemical involved in the sleep process.

In 1987 Dr. David Orme-Johnson of the Maharishi International University, surveyed people who meditated. In the nineteen to thirty-nine year old age group, he discovered that people who meditated were 54.7 percent less likely to require visits to a doctor. In the over forty group, this percentage rose dramatically to 73.7 percent. And the percentage of meditators in all age levels who were admitted to the hospital for heart disease or tumors was extremely low.

With these figures in mind, sick people, caregivers, and healers should make meditation part of their weekly routine. Meditation doesn't have to be practiced every day to work its wonders but should be done at least three times a week. All meditation requires is you, a comfortable straight chair (or a pillow so you can sit on the floor), soft nonvocal music, and five to twenty minutes. I include the soft music because it masks many distracting sounds.

Meditation also produces what is known as an altered state of consciousness. Shamans know that an altered state of consciousness is necessary to heal yourself or another person. You can't force yourself to achieve this. Shamans frequently produce this trancelike state through drums and dancing. Modern meditation allows you to ease gently into an altered state of consciousness in which the physical body is so relaxed that the meditator is no longer aware of it. The consciousness is raised to the level of the eighth and ninth chakras, a place where communication with the Divine is possible and secret universal healing knowledge is available. When you reach this state, you can mold universal energy into any healing form you choose, and the healing will be complete.

Some people like to burn candles or incense while meditating. If you do this, be certain that the candle or incense is in a fireproof container in a safe place well away from anything that could catch fire. Lavender is a good relaxing scent. If you use lavender in an aromatherapy burner, make sure that there is enough water in the container so that the hot oil won't pop out and make a mess or crack the container. If you use incense, don't set it close to you or use it in a small room. The smoke can make you cough or choke. If you don't like incense smoke, place a few drops of lavender oil on a cotton ball in a small dish.

If you feel more comfortable following a guided meditation tape, you can purchase these or make them yourself. Then you can replay the tape whenever you meditate.

I have learned over the years that people in Western cultures find it difficult to practice the Eastern idea of meditation with a blank mind. Paramahansa Yogananda, who started the Self Realization Fellowship years ago, understood this when he tailored the techniques from India to the Western mind.

This is why my meditations in this book and others have guided imagery and suggestions.

Visualization techniques entice your subconscious mind to heal the body. The subconscious mind understands only symbols and pictures, so visualization connects you with it. As the saying goes, change your mind and you change your life. Healing visualizations are also essential if a healer is working on a sick person some distance away, (see chapter 9).

Choose a meditation spot where you will not be disturbed. Play your meditation tape or a soft, non-vocal tape of music. To begin a meditation, sit in a straight-backed chair with your feet flat on the floor and your hands in your lap. If you prefer, you can sit cross-legged on the floor with a pillow under the back portion of your buttocks. This will tip you slightly forward so that you rest on a portion of your knees. If you are ill and in bed, lie flat on your back with a pillow under your knees and another under your head. I don't recommend lying down unless you can't sit because the prone posture is conducive to sleep. If you really want to try a yogic pose for meditation, most people can safely do the half-lotus. Sit cross-legged with one foot on the opposite thigh but the other foot on the floor. Don't use this position if it causes you pain. Meditation isn't about enduring pain but

Half-lotus pose

about relaxing and connecting with the flow of universal energy and information.

You will never be in any spiritual danger while meditating. You can end the meditation simply by opening your eyes. Your body and soul won't be possessed by evil spirits, either.

* * *

Close your eyes and take a slow, deep breath. When you exhale, purse your lips, tighten your body muscles, and blow slowly. This expels any stale air that is in the bottom of your lungs. This exhalation method is also helpful to people who hyperventilate or have asthma. Now relax again and take another slow, deep breath. As you inhale, visualize a bright white light or the sun over your head. See this light filling your body as the breath fills your lungs. When you exhale slowly and normally, this light will wash out all negative energy and emotions within you.

Breathing normally, begin to mentally tell your body to relax, beginning with the feet and legs and ending with the shoulders, neck, and head muscles. Take your time but don't dwell too long on this part of the exercise. If you try too hard to relax, you will defeat your purpose.

After a short time, visualize yourself standing beside a small stream of running water. Take all of your negative emotions and events (including troublesome people) and throw them into the stream. This action tells the subconscious mind that these people and events should be resolved or removed from your life.

You turn away from the stream and see a wall with a door. You go to the door and open it. Inside is an empty room with a chair. On the wall in front of the chair is a huge screen, like a movie screen. You sit in the chair and look at the screen. You will use this screen and the power within this room to build your-self an Otherworld healing temple where you can go to heal yourself or work on healing for others.

Begin building this temple by visualizing on the screen what setting you wish it to be in: on top of a mountain, beside the sea or a lake, in the forest, out on a desert, even on the moon or in the clouds. The set-ting can be anything you wish. Now, mentally con-struct the temple in any shape, of any size, and of any material you wish. You may want it to look like a castle or perhaps like a giant seashell. The choice is yours. Create any windows and doors you want.

Now, go inside your healing temple and decorate the interior in any manner you want. You may wish to have your main healing room within a place of wor-ship, or it may look like a modern house furnished with soft beds for patients or yourself to lie upon. You can come to this Otherworld place anytime you are in meditation, either to be healed, to relax, or to work on healing for another. This is your refuge from stress and your spot to connect with universal energy.

Take as much time as you need to create this sacred space. It will remain intact in the ethereal realms, wait-ing for you whenever you enter meditation.

When you are ready to return to this time and place, open your eyes and move slowly until you are reoriented.

* * *

You can return to your healing temple at any time. Just be certain that you dump the negatives before you go there so you don't contaminate your healing space.

To do healing work in your temple, mentally call the name of the sick person. Their astral body will appear in the temple, and you can begin your work. See chapter 9, "Absent Healing," for more suggestions about healing techniques using meditation. To heal yourself, lie down on one of your healing beds in the temple and call for your spiritual guides, guardian angels, or a deity to help you.

If you experience painful memories while in meditation, acknowledge their existence, but tell yourself that you will not let them control or influence your life. You may need to drop them into the stream several times before your subconscious mind gets the message that you don't need to relive these any longer.

Sometimes, you will get visions of unfamiliar events. These are images from past lives, images that contain clues to present problems and health trouble. If you are healing another person, these unbidden images belong to them. Look closely at these fragmentary events for clues to present life troubles. These past life memories are dealt with the same as those from your past in this life.

At some time during a meditation, you may become aware of something attached to you that you didn't know was there. If healing another person, you may see something attached to them. These are called cordings. Cordings are attachments between people. These cordings may arise in this lifetime or in past lives. Although they appear positive between good friends, lovers, and close family members, they are frequently negative connections that you don't want or need. You may see these in meditation as a rope-like attachment to one or all of your, or the patient's, first three chakras. They are usually dull and muddy in color, although active ones can appear fire-red. You can sever and eliminate these unwanted energy drainers and controllers by visualizing a bright sword or a flaming torch in your power hand. Simply cut or burn the cordings in two. It may take several attempts to completely sever strong cordings.

Your own silver (sometimes a light blue) cord that attaches your astral body (soul) to the physical body is always with you and is not the same as a negative cording. The silver cord can't be suddenly attacked by evil astral entities and severed. It detaches itself when your life is finished, and only then.

It is possible that you will meet spiritual guides, guardian angels, or deceased loved ones while meditating. They want to help you. If they make you uncomfortable, ask them to leave.

If you are working on healing another person while in meditation, be aware of the patient's body language as soon as you make mental contact with them. Some people do not want to be healed but wish to leave the earth plane for a more pain-free existence in the Otherworld. I had this forcefully brought home one time when I was working on the father of a friend. During my meditation, when I contacted the comatose elderly gentleman, who was in the hospital, I immediately saw two images of the man. One was lying quietly on the hospital bed, but the other was actively wielding a kitchen broom, batting away all the healing energy. I had never met the father and was amazed that his spirit body was so active in resistance. When I described the man to my friend, thinking I might have contacted the wrong person, he assured me the description fit his father, who used a kitchen broom to oust both unwanted Texas critters and salesmen. His father had once remarked that if he ever got too sick to live life as he wanted, he didn't want to continue living. So, instead of a healing, I worked for a pain-free, peaceful passage from this life.

Sometimes you may wish to meditate on a more spiritual level without using a guided journey. In this case, you can use mantras and mudras. Mudras, however, can be used in either type of meditation, guided or silent.

A mantra is a single word or a series of words that center and calm the user through their vibrational qualities, (see chapter 6). This word or series of words is chanted with each exhalation of breath while you meditate.

A mudra is a hand gesture that has held a certain meaning for thousands of years. A few of these are explained below. In the ancient Hindu tradition these mudras, or hand gestures, are considered very powerful. Some mudras are also quite elaborate. The ones I list here are simple and can be used easily by anyone during meditation to increase their contact with the spiritual and to amplify healing energy. The Chalice and Gomukha mudras are inconspicuous enough that you can use them at almost any time.

The Namaste mudra is done by holding the palms of the hands flat together, fingers pointing upward, at heart level, as if in prayer. This gesture honors God/Goddess and the spiritual flame within every other person.

The Om mudra is usually made when chanting the mantra "Om (ohm)." In this gesture, you bring the tips of the thumb and index finger of each hand together to form a circle. The hands are rested palms up on the knees.

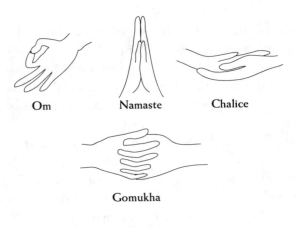

Mudras

The powerful Chalice mudra is usually made while sitting in the half-lotus pose. It represents the receiving of spiritual blessings and healing energy from the Divine. Hold your hands together, slightly cupped. You do this by placing the right hand inside the left. Let the tips of the thumbs touch. If your right foot is on the opposite thigh in the half-lotus, put the right hand inside the left. If your left foot is on the opposite thigh, place the left hand inside the right. Hold your hands just below your navel.

The Gomukha mudra is a powerful gesture to use when your energy feels scattered and you are having difficulty concentrating. Interlace the fingers of both hands while holding one thumb on top of the other. Hold your hands in your lap.

Combine the mudras with chants and affirmations from chapter 6, and you will greatly enhance both your meditations and their results.

Often, physical visual effects are helpful during a meditation. The person meditating can look at certain symbols before and after a meditation to help produce an altered state of consciousness. Some healers make healing altars and have candles and clear quartz crystals placed around a photo or paper bearing the patient's name. See chapter 13 for more on healing altars. The same technique can be used in absent healing.

If you want to intensify and strengthen your meditations, place certain tarot cards and stones where you can see them before and after a healing meditation. If you have a photo of the sick person, place this in the center of your cards and stones. If you don't have a photo, write the patient's full name on a piece of paper instead.

If you use one tarot card, place a stone on each side of it or surround it with stones. If you use several tarot cards, alternate the cards and stones around the photo or name of the sick person. The following lists of cards and stones give their healing meanings so you can determine which you want to use. The stones are all inexpensive and easily found.

TAROT CARDS

The Chariot: self-discipline, willpower, forging ahead

The Empress: the Goddess or Mary, compassion, emotional order, good luck

Four of Swords: rest, recuperation, quiet contemplation, regrouping of energy

The Hermit: peace in solitude, hidden knowledge brought to light

Nine of Cups: wishes granted

Six of Swords: journeying away from problems, improved situation

Six of Wands: victory

The Star: balance and harmony, peace, spiritual enlightenment

Strength: inner control of emotions and problems, harnessing inner strength

The Sun: good health, enlightenment, healing

Temperance: brings harmony, balance, and tranquility

Ten of Cups: joy and contentment, complete happiness, permanent success

HEALING STONES

Agate, red: This stone brings peace and calmness, and aids in healing blood diseases.

Amber: This stone soothes and heals. It increases the strength of your healing spells and meditations.

Amethyst: This stone helps strengthen your communication with your spiritual teachers and guardians. It also aids in achieving the altered state of consciousness.

Carnelian: This stone strengthens and energizes the blood and internal organs. It also aids in regenerating damaged tissue.

Hematite: This stone releases stress and brings in optimism, will, and courage.

Lapis lazuli: This stone is one of the greatest healers and purifiers. It helps reduce tension and stress, as well as balance the chakras.

Malachite: This stone heals the heart and circulatory system, revitalizes the body and mind, and regenerates tissue. It also stabilizes the energy and heals the chakras.

Onyx, black: This stone deflects and destroys negative energy, particularly the kind sent by others. It aids with spiritual inspiration, balancing karmic debt, and helps when facing transformational events.

Quartz crystal, clear: This stone is a great healer and also amplifies all healing energy.

Quartz, rose: This stone helps heal emotional wounds and release negative emotions. It attracts universal love and healing energies.

A good healer is always searching for new methods of healing. If you are interested in making your own healing weapons, for example, I suggest you read Michael Smith's books: *Crystal Power, Crystal Spirit,* and *Crystal Warrior.* He gives full details for healing wands and other useful items.

Never give up hope and never stop your healing work for yourself or a patient. When it seems the darkest, a change is often right around the corner. Willpower directed through a healing meditation is very powerful. It can also be a spiritually uplifting experience for the patient, the caregiver, and the healer.

CHAPTER SIX

Affirmations and Chants

AFFIRMATIONS

Healers of all ages, past and present, have known that the patient's will to recover and the will to live are essential for a healing. Sick people can die quickly of a non-fatal disease if they give up hope and believe they will die. We see this combination of illness and despair more and more, because modern medicine has separated the body from the mind and spirit in healing. You would think we would learn to reinforce modern medicine with ancient alternative practices that will heal the entire person, on all levels. Without healing a patient on all levels, there can be no complete healing.

There are physicians who believe in the connection between irresponsible or negative thinking and illnesses. One physician I know insists that his patients become responsible for their diseases. Although his definition of being responsible and mine are not quite the same, we have definitely established a way of understanding each other.

It is the responsibility of patients and their families to take active roles in healing. The easiest method is to use positive affirmations, which are short sentences, without negative words. For example, don't say, "George doesn't have cancer." Instead, say, "George is completely healed." And hold a mental picture of George happy and healthy. If a negative thought does arise, immediately counter it by saying, "I don't accept that!"

Never speak of a disease as a reality unless this is counteracted by positive words, for this sets into motion disintegrating forces within the body, mind, and spirit. Instead of claiming a disease, speak of it as the disease, not *my* cold, or *George's* cancer.

Negative thoughts, words, and attitudes have become so much a part of human life that they arise without our being aware of them. However, the subconscious mind recognizes these and acts upon them. The subconscious reaction to negatives appears first in the aura, then in the body in the form of diseases. If you say something negative about an illness or disease, or someone says something negative to you, immediately and mentally say, "No, I don't accept that." Then replace it with "I (or the patient's name) am getting well."

The ancient Egyptians and the Brahmins of India knew the power of negative words and thoughts. They deliberately used certain healing words to set up vibratory actions that could help heal broken bones and depleted internal organs. They used prolonged sessions of healing chants to stimulate the glands and nerve centers. The healers of India believed that spoken or sung words were 80 percent more powerful than the same words spoken only in the mind. Hindu scriptures say that words are all-powerful. The ancient Babylonians taught that every word is a command or a promise that must come true. The Greeks believed that words contained power and cosmic energy to build up or tear down. Oriental cultures have long taught that the spoken word has tremendous power, and that certain arrangements of words (as in healing affirmations and chants) can profoundly affect physical substance.

These ideas were not used in Europe after the terror of the witch hunts, for the wise men and women who knew these secrets were killed or had gone into deep hiding and no longer served the people. However, spiritual healing secrets never stay hidden forever. Eventually, people begin to rediscover and use them.

Around the turn of the nineteenth century, a French pharmacist named Emile Coué had a free clinic where he taught patients to use positive affirmations. One of these affirmations has survived and is still used today: "Every day in every way, I am getting better and better." His patients who repeated this twenty times when they awoke each morning did get better. He chose morning because affirmations work best when the patient is relaxed and calm.

In 1964 Norman Cousins, author of *Anatomy of an Illness*, learned he had a deadly form of arthritis that attacks the body's connective tissues. His chances of surviving more than a few months were not good. Determined not to give up, he began to fill his life with a positive attitude, positive speech, and lots of humor. In four months he was back to work full-time, although his complete cure took several years. Mr. Cousins had instinctively used the ancient healing technique of positive affirmations and thinking, and proved that it works.

Mental thoughts also affect the body, mind, and spirit. Repeated imagining of negative thoughts produces a powerful astral thoughtform that the subconscious mind takes as a literal wish. Robert Monroe, author of *Ultimate Journey*, did research on this in the 1970s. He coined the term "H-Band" noise to describe the thought pollution of negative thoughts created by undisciplined human mental imagining and negative speech. This pollution surrounds us constantly. And this, combined with negative words and thoughts can have an extremely detrimental affect on a sick person's health.

Negative-speaking and -thinking people are detrimental to your health. Avoid them, when possible. This includes people who are always complaining, making excuses, blaming others for their actions, and finding fault with others. Life is difficult enough without added problems, so choose your companions carefully.

You need to rid yourself of secret resentment, anger, or despair over past injustices. Begin by using affirming statements that tell your subconscious mind to solve these problems and kick out the negative debris. Even if you can't bring yourself to be around someone who harmed you in some manner, at least heal yourself by changing your thinking. For example, say aloud in private: "I forgive (name) for what she/he did (or said), but I have no need for (name) in my life. He/she is free to pay whatever karmic debts are owed in some other way, but not to me." From experience I know this will take time, sometimes a long time, but it can be done. The release of this negative debris will improve your life and health. It is the first step to true healing. You must do this yourself, for no one else can do it for you.

Cancer is a difficult disease for orthodox modern medicine to cure. It is also a difficult disease for psychic healers and may require many treatments over a long period of time. With cancer, more than any other disease, patients must truthfully look at their life and thoughts, and make changes. Many cancer patients refuse to discuss their feelings. However, they may be seething inwardly with anger, power, control, betrayal, or other emotional traumas. The aura's layers may hold the beginnings of this disease for years before the problem reaches the physical body.

When cancer is still in the aura's layers, healers may find intense hot spots that will burn their hands with flares of excess energy or see it as a black area with coruscating red dots flashing in it. This black spot will be perpendicular to the body where it will eventually manifest unless rooted out. The closer to the body the spot is in the aura, the more compacted the disease is and the sooner it may manifest. All cancers already in the body will show this dark area and the aura will feel extremely hot there. Although the healer may work on the aura, the patient must perform self-healing by affirmations and positive visualizations to attack and eradicate this disease.

Ancient healers knew about cancer, but not to the extent we know of it today. They were also aware that people can become predisposed to the disease through bottled-up negative emotions.

Dr. Masaharu Taniguchi, a Japanese metaphysician and successful cancer healer, believed that pessimism, resentments, fault-finding, and criticism were detrimental to good health.

Many psychic healers and metaphysicians believe that cancer may be caused by holding onto some secret resentment, anger, or bitterness.

The first time I saw clearly the connection between cancer and bitterness/resentment was in the case of a woman in her late thirties. Lucille had little love in her childhood. She had been deliberately pushed aside for her two younger siblings. She married young to a cruel, manipulative man who abused her physically and mentally. He was also an alcoholic woman-izer who sexually abused his daughter. His son was a copy of his father. Through all of this, Lucille presented a sweet, lov-ing face to the world, rarely criticizing and stoutly defending her family. In actuality, she was afraid to have her husband ar-rested because he threatened to kill her, and the daughter was using the incestuous relationship to gain material objects she wanted. Lucille kept her resentment and rage bottled up in-side. At age thirty-four she was diagnosed with breast cancer and had a mastectomy. Three years later, she had a small lump and cancer recurred at the mastectomy site; these were treated with radiation therapy. A year later, she was diagnosed with advanced bone cancer in the skull and hips. When her ex-hausted body and spirit finally gave up, she died at age thirty-nine. The irony of the entire situation was the husband jokingly spoke of long-term anger producing cancer, but he completely absolved himself of any wrongdoing and blamed it on his wife's parents.

If you hold on to a negative past and injustices done to you, you are poisoning your aura and body. This type of attitude attracts more such negative experiences your way, adding to the debris piling up within your aura until a disease will at last erupt in the physical body.

Anyone, regardless of their religious background, can use affirmations, which are about health, not religion. If you want a religious-based practice, however, you can use prayer. Prayer is simply a form of spiritual affirmation that can bring about healing changes.

Repeat a healing affirmation over and over, even if you don't believe at first. This will raise your subconscious thinking and change your body. By repeating a verbal affirmation over and over, the subconscious mind gets the message and acts upon it. This produces a profound effect on the auras, the physical body, and the mind. If you can picture the healing within your mind, you can hold it in your hand. However, patients must picture this healing for themselves. No healer can, or should, try to force a healing on a patient who will not cooperate and take part in getting well.

In magic, a chant or spell repeated three times is considered more powerful. Repeating affirmations at least three times will amplify the desire you are sending out. The more often you say an affirmation, the stronger it gets. If you will speak an affirmation forty-nine times and hold the desired image in your mind with each affirmation, you can gain the result.

For those people who don't feel comfortable making up their own affirmations, the following list may help.

- I forgive all who have done me harm and step forward into a new and better life.
- Every day in every way, I am getting better and better.
- I am completely healed of all disease on all levels of my body.
- I am well. I am whole. I am happy.
- My body, mind, and spirit are filled with healing light and energy.
- I am one with God/Goddess and healed of all afflictions.
- I claim complete healing and believe that it will be so.

CHANTS AND MANTRAS

Chanting has been a vital part of religion and healing sessions for thousands of years in almost every culture. Frequently, chanting was combined with music, as with the Gregorian chants of the early Christian churches and monasteries. Today, the Gregorian chants are available on cassette tapes or CD.

The Gregorian chant, although Christian in origin, can transcend religious barriers and bring peace and harmony to any listener. Chants are capable of bridging the sacred and the secular, and thus help you to attain an altered state of consciousness. This altered state of consciousness brings both the chanter and the listener closer to the Otherworld realms and healing power.

Ancient deities of music were often associated with healing as well. An example is the god Apollo, who was a deity of both music and healing. The Greek god Aesculapius was Apollo's son and considered to be a great healer.

Words are simply a blend of vowels and consonants. These vowels and consonants have long been considered words that have a universal meaning. The sounds are a bridge between languages and cultures. The priest-magicians and healers of many ancient cultures, such as the Egyptians, Babylonians, Hindus, Orientals, and Greeks, studied the power and effect of certain sounds, particularly when chanted with intent. They discovered that, without directed intent, words and sounds would accomplish nothing. Only toning or chanting with intent will balance and heal.

The healers and magicians of the past knew that these sounds had vast reservoirs of power for magic and healing. At first, this knowledge was the sole property of the temples.

However, the priest-magicians and healers later taught this information to the people through the use of chants and mantras. Frequently, the chants and mantras were only a special combination of sounds that had no literal meaning, but were chosen for their healing effects.

Scientists have not completely explored the power of sound. We know that certain sounds have a visible effect on objects. A high-pitched sound will shatter glass, and certain levels of sound will rearrange fine sand into subtle patterns. We also know that noises measuring ninety decibels or more can double the heart rate. Still, modern medicine does not accept that chanting and the use of mantras can help heal.

When mantras are mentioned, people immediately think of the Hindu religion. However, both the Buddhists and Hindus have used mantras in meditation for centuries. They believe that the sounds of certain mantras, when used repeatedly, can heal and positively influence events. Ancient Hindu texts state that the mantra "Om" is the most powerful mystic sound, and when repeated many times can harmonize the body and spirit with the cosmos. This scripture also says that certain *bija* mantras (called seed mantras) correspond to and affect the seven chakras.

Most people are not aware that the Sufi religion has a deep respect for, and uses, the power of sound. The Sufis practice deep breathing, chanting, and mantras as a vital part of their religion. Their word *ghiza-i-rhu*, which translates to music, really means food for the soul. To them, singing increases *prana* or *ch'i*, which is life energy. They also use chanting to achieve an altered state of consciousness, much as shamans do, and say that there is true healing power in the sounds of chanting. The Sufis frequently use the *bija* mantras (discussed later in this chapter) to focus and calm the mind, just as the Hindus do.

By saying mantras, you can switch on the chakras safely and make them operate at full power. Even if you don't understand what you are saying, these ancient formulas work because mantras are fundamentally about energy rather than meaning. Mantras are a single word or a series of words that were chosen for their vibrational and centering qualities. Mantras help you to reach the eighth and ninth chakras, the doorways to ch'i, or cosmic energy. The more you say a mantra, the more power you can tap. When you focus the sound vibration of a mantra with a consciously held intent, you can direct its energy to whatever portion of the body you choose. Mantras can also burn off karma.

Numbers and sounds are also connected in ancient lore. The sixth-century Greek philosopher Pythagoras studied sound and numbers for years, especially the number nine. The number nine had great significance in ancient healing ceremonies, as it was considered a complete number and capable of creation. Any number that was a multiple of nine was also considered powerful.

The Hindus recommend a forty-day repetition of a mantra for maximum benefit. However, few people can set aside forty days for constant mantra repetition. Instead of being overwhelmed by the idea of forty days of chanting, you can choose to say a mantra for a specific number of times.

If you are striving for a set number of repetitions a day, you can keep count by using a *mala*, a rosary-like object that originated in the Far East. It is composed of one hundred eight beads. The Vedic *malas*, later used by the Buddhists, existed for thousands of years before the Catholic rosary was first used. Twenty rosaries equal ten *malas*, a good number of repetitions to use for a specific prayer or mantra.

Malas can be purchased at specialty shops or through catalogs and are not expensive. The one bead at the end of the *mala* is called the *meru*. Hindus say that the *meru* contains the accumulated power of all the mantras performed. The Sanskrit word *meru* means mountain of stored energy. Never cross over the *meru* when you go around the *mala*. To continue chanting the mantra, start the count again by going backward from the *meru*.

Hindu Ayurvedic medicine uses the power of the voice to balance and align chakras through reciting mantras. However, you can also use related vowel sounds.

It is not necessary to sing your chants or mantras unless you wish to do so. You don't have to sing a certain note or in a certain key, either. When chanting either vowels and consonants or mantras, the patient or healer should take a slow, deep breath, and chant while slowly exhaling. The sounds should be in your ordinary, natural voice. When done properly, the sound should vibrate in your head.

Never chant on a full stomach when your body's energy is primarily concentrated on digestion. Wait at least an hour after eating so your body will be more receptive. Also, relax your body as much as possible. This will enable you to breathe naturally and produce vibrating tones. Sit with your back straight, whether you sit in a chair or cross-legged on the floor. This will allow the cosmic energy you are enticing into your body to penetrate all chakras and meridians. If the energy can't penetrate all portions of your aura and all of your chakras, it can't flow unimpeded along the meridians. Thus, the cosmic healing energy won't do the best job.

Certain vowels and consonants historically have been linked to certain results. These vowels and consonants are known to all cultures and are in all languages. If you aren't comfortable with the mantras given later in this chapter, at least use the vowels and consonants. The following sounds can help with healing.

The *a* sound, as in "ahh," can help with depression. It also helps the body assimilate more oxygen, which causes the brain to release endorphins, substances that aid in natural pain control.

The long *e* sound, as in "emit" or "feel," stimulates the pineal gland and arouses the body's energies.

The short *e*, as in "echo," affects the thyroid gland, increasing the metabolism and secretion of hormones. This is useful for patients who have lost their appetites and aren't eating properly.

The long *o*, as in "ocean," can be used to control sugar cravings, for it stimulates the pancreas. This sound will also help create a connection between the toner and the environment.

Intone the *oo* sound, as in "tool," to stimulate the spleen. This stimulation will build the immune system. It also aids in bridging the conscious and subconscious minds.

The *mmm* sound is connected with the Goddess. Today, Her counterpart in orthodox religion is the Virgin Mary. This sound, when vibrated through the physical body into the astral body, will create balance on all levels.

The *shh* sound made by mothers the world over can restore harmony and peace.

Using vowel sounds to balance the chakras will not overload or unbalance any of these light centers. The *uh* sound, as in "huh," works on the root chakra, while the *ooo*, as in "fool," affects the belly chakra. The *oh*, as in "low," will clear the solar plexus chakra, while the *ah*, as in "hah," will benefit the heart chakra. The sound *eye* is for the throat chakra, and the long *a*, as in "hay," will help the brow chakra, also known as the Third Eye. The long *e*, as in "feel," will benefit the crown chakra at the top of the head.

Certain combinations of sounds can also be used together to attain specific goals. Spells for love and relationship are affected by "ahh eh," a combination of Mother and Father sonics. "Shoo maa" will help manifest material goals, while "paa maa eye oh" strengthens protective spells. These sample combinations may also be combined with the *bija* mantras and chakra mantras that follow.

If you wish to work primarily on the chakras themselves, the following mantras will aid you. They are easily pronounced one-word mantras. Sit with your back straight. Place your power hand over each chakra and visualize its color as you chant the mantra. Remember to breathe in and then chant while you exhale. Begin with the root chakra and end with the brow chakra. The crown chakra doesn't have a mantra associated with it. When the other six chakras are cleared and balanced, the totality of the sounds of these six resonate in the seventh chakra.

Mantras for the chakras are:

Lam (lahm)—root chakra

Vam (vahm)—belly chakra

Ram (rahm)—solar plexus chakra

Yam (yahm)—heart chakra

Hum (hoom)—throat chakra

Om (ohm)—brow chakra

Work with a seed mantra for at least ten days, repeating it as often as possible. Do the same with the chakra mantras but chant all of them, one after the other in the correct order, each time you say them.

Bija mantras, also called seed mantras, are one-word Hindu mantras that are used for specific purposes. You can combine them with chakra mantras or vowel and consonant sounds. The seed mantras are the simplest of Hindu mantras and the easiest to chant.

Shrim (shreem): This affects the energy of abundance in all forms and is connected with the goddess Lakshmi. It also helps with spiritual abundance, health, inner peace, financial wealth, friendship, and love of children and family. According to Vedic teaching, if you say *shrim* one hundred times, your experiences of abundance will increase a hundredfold.

Eim (I'm): This rules artistic and scientific endeavors, music, education, and spiritual endeavors. It is connected with the goddess Sarasvati.

Klim (kleem): This seed mantra is often combined with other mantras to attract an object of desire.

Dum (doom): This invokes the energy of protection.

Gum (as in chewing gum): This mantra is connected with the god Ganesha, who removes obstacles and brings success to endeavors.

Glaum (glah-own): This removes obstacles that may exist between the throat and the base of the spine in both the physical and astral bodies. It is connected with Ganesha.

Haum (how, with an m added): Connected with the god Shiva, this mantra greatly affects contact with the transcendental consciousness that is found in the eighth and ninth chakras.

Kshraum (unvocalized k with sh, followed by row [how] and an "m"): Connected with the god Vishnu, this mantra is used to be rid of the most stubborn evil situations and to release pent-up energies.

Hrim (hreem): This helps see through the illusions of everyday life. It can put you in contact with the higher spiritual realms where spiritual teachers, guardian angels, and exalted beings dwell.

Unless a patient is unconscious or totally unable to make a sound, mantras and chants can be used. Even if the patient must whisper, the power of these ancient mantras will draw in healing power from the cosmos.

CHAPTER SEVEN

Tonal and Musical Healing

Ancient cultures fully understood the power within music. They used music to create receptive attitudes during religious worship and healing atmospheres for the sick. We can see the effects of military-type music, which can produce national fervor and a militant attitude. Mothers have used lullabies for centuries to help their children sleep.

In ancient times, musicians were valuable members of society and often combined their talents with healing. We find references to this in writings from ancient Egypt and Greece. Celtic bards were prohibited from creating the wrong attitude in their audiences.

Today, doctors are beginning to accept that certain forms of music are conducive to healing, whether it is patients playing or listening to music. Many people are familiar with Don Campbell's book, *The Mozart Effect*, in which he discusses the modern scientific studies done with music and the results that were found. This book made many parents more watchful about the types of music their children listen to. Gregorian chant was found to be excellent for quiet study and meditation and can reduce stress. Slower baroque music can produce a sense of stability and order; examples are certain compositions by Bach, Handel, and Vivaldi. Classical music, such as that of Haydn and Mozart, can improve concentration and memory. Compositions by the New Age musician Stephen Halpern were specifically written to help bring about positive results.

Beyond creating a harmonious environment for learning and evolving, tone and sound can produce powerful effects on cells and tissue, and even help shrink malignant growths. While there are few modern studies of these effects, ancient healers were adamant about this healing effect.

One of the newest methods of using musical tones to heal involves tuning forks. You may buy tuning forks in a special set of eight that comes with a protective cloth bag with individual compartments for each fork. The cloth bag can be rolled up and tied to protect them. (See the appendix for product suppliers.)

In tone, these tuning forks go from middle C up an octave to C. Basically, these forks correspond to each of the eight chakras, beginning with middle C and the root chakra, and working up to the transpersonal chakra and the next C. The sounds produced by the tuning forks work in two ways. First, the auditory senses transfer the sound to the body, aura, and chakras through the ears. Second, the sound waves produced by the vibrating forks can directly transfer moving energy to the chakras, aura, or parts of the body. To use the tuning forks, hold one gently by the stem. Tap it lightly against the block provided with the set. Don't hit a tuning fork against a hard surface or ever strike them with great force.

You can use tuning forks to cleanse the chakras and aura in several ways. If you discover a flare, depression, or any other anomaly in the patient's aura, you can choose a tuning fork that corresponds to the chakra that controls that area of the body. Strike the fork and hold it near the damaged or diseased area. Then, seal the aura with the hands. If the problem persists, the healer should cleanse the chakras and then go back to the damaged area and try again. Sometimes, holding a tuning fork near the end of a quartz crystal that is pointed at the area will amplify the energy.

To cleanse the chakras, begin with the largest fork, middle C. Strike the fork, hold it over the root chakra, and visualize the color red. When the fork stops vibrating, move to the next fork and the belly chakra. Continue this procedure until you have worked your way up to the transpersonal chakra, which lies just above the head. You may also chant the appropriate vowel/consonant or mantra while doing this. If you wish, you

Use of tuning forks on the body

can also sing or hum the tone while working with the tuning forks.

In healing, if you discover that two chakras are connected with an illness, you can choose the appropriate tuning forks for those two chakras and strike both at the same time. Holding the vibrating forks in the aura should aid in attacking stubborn, persistent, or severe illness.

If the exact site of an illness is known, the healer can apply the vibrating tones of the tuning fork directly to that area. Be certain that you understand which chakra controls that area and/or disease so that you can use the correct tuning fork.

If two healers are working on a patient at the same time, one healer can work on the aura with the hands, while the other strikes and uses the tuning forks. This is a bit difficult if

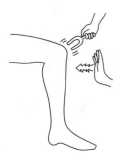

Toning and using of hands

you are applying this technique to your own body, but with a little practice, it can be done in most areas.

Tuning forks are also useful to create an altered state of consciousness in some healers and patients. When doing this, two tuning forks are used at the same time. Middle C and D will project an outer calming vibration that is soothing to the atmosphere and the patient. Middle C and B affect the mind and nervous system for an inner calming. Middle C and E produce an atmosphere of outer energy, while middle C and A produce an inner energy. This last set of forks should be used with great care so that neither the patient nor the healer becomes uncomfortably energized. Middle C and G vibrate mental activity and inspiration into the surrounding atmosphere, while middle C and F provide personal and inner inspiration. Middle C and the higher C affect the etheric levels and often aid in deep meditations and spiritual enlightenment. Some psychics claim that middle C and A are conducive to mystical inspiration. However, I have found that middle C and the higher C work much better for this.

One can also use the tones of tuning forks during magical spells, such as candle burning, making healing poppets, making colored elixirs, creating talismans, and such. This will increase the spell energy, often giving a boost that the healer-magician needs to heal successfully. The following list may be helpful. You can also experiment to see if different tones work better for you on specific spells.

Middle C: This tone strengthens the willpower and the desire to survive. It helps increase physical energy, love, conception, brings success in any desire or project. It also is good for any diseases affected by the root chakra.

D: This tone can change your luck. It helps you accept responsibility and get rid of negative situations. It is good for any diseases affected by the belly chakra.

E: This tone helps you protect yourself from emotional events, understand upsetting life events, remove unrealistic fears, get your life in order. It is good for any diseases affected by the solar plexus chakra.

F: This tone helps you learn to accept life and move gently through it, establish a connection with nature spirits and other ethereal beings, determine your place and purpose in this lifetime. It is good for any diseases affected by the heart chakra.

G: This tone helps you gain confidence for public appearances or duties, learn to stand up for yourself, expand your knowledge, and gain proficiency in your chosen career or in magical endeavors. It is good for any diseases affected by the throat chakra.

A: This tone helps you open the Third Eye, expand your knowledge and use of the psychic, learn to heal yourself and others, seek the right spiritual path. It is good for any diseases affected by the brow chakra.

B: This tone helps you expand your spiritual growth, make contact with your spiritual teachers, guardian spirits, and Goddess/God. It is good for any diseases affected by the crown chakra.

Higher C: This tone helps you seek the ultimate source of spiritual knowledge and power, and establish a universal connection with all things spiritual. There are no diseases, except deep spiritual diseases, associated with the eighth chakra.

Music in all its forms is healing for both the patient and the healer, indeed, for everyone. Choose your music wisely and avoid negative forms of this art, forms that have detrimental effects on the body, mind, and spirit.

CHAPTER EIGHT

Color Healing

We have ancient records detailing how priests in Egypt, Babylonia, and China used colored light in their healing practices. Healing through sunlight therapy was a common medical practice for relief of skin disorders, such as psoriasis, in Greece, China, and Rome. In the late 1890s, Nobel prizewinner Dr. Neils Finsen expanded upon this ancient knowledge and learned how to heal skin lesions using red and infrared light treatments. In 1920, Dinshah Ghadiali from India developed a color healing system that he called Spectro-Chrome. Through experience he determined what colors were most effective in treating a variety of diseases. Today, dermatologists frequently use ultraviolet phototherapy for certain skin disorders.

However, not more than fifty years ago, the Food and Drug Administration banned the use of colored light in healing, saying it was quackery. Now, the government has approved a device, developed by Dr. John Downing, called the

Lumatron which uses colors and light frequencies for therapy. Dr. Jacob Liberman, another pioneering light therapist, called light the medicine of the future because it directly affects the cells.

Today it is possible to buy special light projectors for use in healing, but these machines are expensive. You can make your own projector by using a snap-clip on the end of a small metal rod and fastening this rod so that it extends in front of an ordinary lamp. Make certain the rod is long enough so the plastic is not too close to the heat of the lamp. This device enables you to change colors easily when treating yourself or a patient. Cut out adequately sized squares of colored photo lens plastic and clip whatever color you want to use in front of the lamp. The patient sits at a comfortable distance from the lamp and relaxes for five to ten minutes while soaking up the rays. You don't have to look at the light to benefit from it.

Another method of color light projection requires a small penlight flashlight and squares of colored photo lens plastic. You can use the same colored squares mentioned in chapter 3 for balancing the chakras. Place the appropriate color in the palm of the patient's power hand and shine the light onto the plastic for two minutes at a time. The receiving chakra in the palm of the hand will transfer the power of the color directly into the aura and the chakras.

The color technique can also be used in various visualization techniques. The healer mentally creates balls of energy of specified colors with the hands and then applies these balls of energy directly to the patient's body and aura. Chanting while visualizing will strengthen the power of the colors. If you are doing absent healing, as in chapter 9, you can create balls of colored light-energy in meditation. You can then apply these balls of light to yourself or send them to a patient.

Another ancient color technique is becoming popular today—color-infused water. Water charged with color is sold on the market under the following names: rubio for red; ambero for orange and yellow; verdio for green; ceruleo for blue; and purpuro for indigo and purple. Or you can make your own color-charged water.

To color-charge water, fill a clean, sterilized jar with pure water that contains no additives such as fluoride. Tape a sheet of photo lens plastic of a specific color to a window with the jar of clear water behind it. Another method is to tape the sheet of lens plastic directly to the jar and make certain that the sun strikes the colored plastic. The sun shines through the window and the film onto the jar of water. Let the jar of water stand for one to four hours and then refrigerate. Without refrigeration, it loses its charge in three or four days. Read the color descriptions that follow to determine how to use color-charged water.

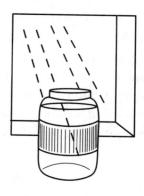

Making color-infused water

For example, take a few sips of orange-charged water before meals for constipation.

The water can be sipped in small amounts, such as a quarter of a cup at a time, two or three times a day. It may also be added to bath water.

To make stronger elixirs, set the jar of water out on a specific planetary day. Sunday is the Sun's day, or yellow, orange, or gold. Monday is the Moon's day, or white or light blue. Tuesday is Mars's day, and is good for red or magenta. Wednesday is Mercury's day, or orange, lemon, or yellow. Thursday is Jupiter's day, or violet, purple, turquoise, or dark blue. Friday is Venus's day, or green or pink. Saturday is Saturn's day, or dark purple or indigo.

You can charge your elixirs with greater power by using tuning forks, (see chapter 7). When the elixir is finished, and you have poured it into the properly labeled bottle for storage, strike the appropriate tuning fork and hold it close to the bottle. The following list will help you decide which tuning fork to use.

Middle C: red, magenta
D: orange
E: yellow, lemon, gold
F: green, pink
G: blue
A: indigo, turquoise
B: violet, purple
Higher C: white and clear quartz crystal elixirs only (See gem
 elixirs in the following pages.)

The following list of colors will help you determine which colors you should use for certain diseases or illnesses. Frequently, more than one color can be used for healing a specific disease. In this case, choose the color that your intuition says is best or treat the patient with several different colors. If you decide to use more than one color, allow at least an hour between treatment with one color and treatment with another color. Never combine the light colors for one treatment. If you are using color-infused water, have the patient take the doses separately, half an hour apart.

You will notice that some of the colors state that they should be followed by treatment with another specific color for certain diseases. This is to strengthen the treatment or to minimize side effects from the first color.

You will also notice that some colors are not recommended for specific diseases because they have a negative effect on those diseases.

Blue: A calming color for the nervous system, blue reduces fear and rapid heartbeat, and cures insomnia. It can also be used for burns, itching, painful skin abrasions, apoplexy, biliousness, cataracts, glaucoma, chicken pox, colic, diarrhea, fever, laryngitis, sore throat, dysentery, eye inflammation, gastrointestinal diseases, hysteria, painful menstruation, heart palpitations, goiter, headache, acute rheumatism, shock, toothache, tonsillitis, duodenal ulcers, vomiting, and jaundice. It is particularly useful in localizing and limiting the destructive effects in the areas around tumors. Because of its sedative qualities, blue also helps with pain. When using blue to treat gastric and duodenal ulcers, asthma, pleurisy, cystic mastitis, diarrhea, and prostate enlargement, follow this color with orange. Do not use blue on colds, constriction of muscles, hypertension, or paralysis.

Gold: A combination of orange and yellow, this color can revitalize the entire nervous system, as well as increase vitality and energy.

Green: This color stimulates the pituitary gland and is useful in treating dysfunction of that gland. It also helps rebuild damaged muscles and body tissues, disinfect, detoxify, and dissolve growths. Use green for ulcers, cancer, asthma, back disorders, head colds, colic, hay fever, high blood pressure, irritability, laryngitis, malaria, malignancies, nervous diseases, neuralgia, and sleeplessness. However, there is a difference of opinion on using this color to treat heart disease, some saying it is not advisable. Personally, I find it works fine for heart problems. If in doubt, use pink and pale violet instead. Use green followed by magenta when treating toxicity caused by problems in the colon, liver, or kidneys. Use with orange to loosen up and removed diseased etheric matter in the aura.

Indigo: This combination of blue and violet light will increase white blood cell counts, stimulate the pituitary gland, and help with blood purification. It also helps with cataracts, appendicitis, asthma, bronchitis, hearing loss, cataracts, convulsions, dyspepsia, hyperthyroidism, all lung problems, nervous ailments, nasal trouble, nosebleed, tonsillitis, and various types of pain. Follow it with gold when treating sinus infections, spine and lower back pain, angina, headaches, hepatitis, and inflammation of the small intestine.

Lemon: This combination of yellow and green is helpful in treating persistent or chronic medical disorders that have not responded to other forms of alternative healing. It also aids in strengthening bones, coughing, dissolving blood clots, and stimulating the immune system.

Magenta: A combination of red and violet, this color helps with many emotional problems. Follow it with green when treating tumors of the pituitary, lungs, breast, stomach, colon, kidneys, uterus, and testicles. Also use it with green for breast cysts, detached retina, tinnitus or ringing in the ears, and water retention.

Orange: This color helps with regeneration of lung tissue and stimulates the thyroid gland. It benefits the entire respiratory system, helps muscle spasms and abdominal cramps, and is useful in treating ovarian cysts, uterine fibroids, and prostate diseases. It is also a good color for gallstones, emphysema, and bronchitis. This color helps with the elimination of waste, toxins, and germs from the body and diseased ethereal matter from the aura. Use orange for asthma, bronchitis, rheumatism, colds, epilepsy, gallstones, malignant and benign growths (particularly in the pre-cancerous stages), hyperthyroidism, hypothyroidism, the lungs, mental exhaustion, and kidney ailments.

Pink: This color is good for emotional healing and to promote self-nurturing.

Purple: This dark, potent color will induce relaxation and promote sleep, as well as lower the body temperature, decrease the blood pressure, and slow the heart rate. It is also useful in treating the kidneys, lungs, and stomach.

Red: This color stimulates the sensory nervous system and the liver and causes regeneration, increases the red blood cell production, and helps with circulation. Red causes rapid tissue and cellular repair and helps with all types of wounds and broken bones. Use for anemia, blood ailments, colds (if no fever), constipation, weight loss, the endocrine system, melancholia, pneumonia, and tuberculosis. Red stimulates the elimination of toxins from the body through the skin, so never treat the patient for more than five minutes at a time. Because red can induce anger in susceptible people, you should take great care when using it. Watch the patient closely for any signs of agitation. In most cases, red is most beneficial when followed by blue or white. Do not use red for nervousness, mentally disturbed people, hypertension, inflammatory conditions, neuritis, asthma, high blood pressure, heart disease, or epilepsy.

Turquoise: This color is obtained by combining green and blue filters in a projection lamp. It affects the thymus gland, which is the major immune center of the body. It is helpful for burns, chronic fatigue syndrome, AIDS, and inflammatory problems. When followed by red, it aids in treating acute sore throat, ear infections, nephritis, and bladder infections.

Violet: An extremely potent color, violet (as well as purple) can be used on severe health problems and diseases, because it promotes rapid healing of damaged internal organs. This color stimulates the spleen and immune systems and will depress the activity of heart muscle, the lymph glands, and the pancreas. It is also useful for painful sciatica, bladder trouble, bone growth, cerebrospinal meningitis, concussion, cramps, kidneys, epilepsy, mental disorders, neuralgia, rheumatism, and tumors. It can increase the white blood cell count and help tranquilize the nervous system.

This color is useful in treating any spiritual disease, as well as helping with headaches and mental disorders.

White: This color actually contains all other colors and is milder than the colors themselves. Therefore, it is very useful in treating infants, young children, the elderly, and extremely ill patients. You can also use it for any disease or at any time to charge the aura's field.

Yellow: A stimulant of the motor nervous system (the neuro-muscular system), this color helps regenerate damaged nerves, stimulates the lymphatic system and intestinal tract, and breaks down deposits in arthritis. It is also useful in treating skin wounds and broken bones, soothing stomach and liver problems, and in increasing positive cellular growth. Use yellow for constipation, diabetes, digestive problems, eczema, flatulence, kidney trouble, indigestion, the liver, mental depression, rheumatism, and the spleen. For paralysis or dysfunction of the nervous system, use yellow followed by violet on the soles of the feet, where there are spinal-reflex points. Do not use yellow for acute inflammation, delirium, diarrhea, fever, neuralgia, or heart palpitations.

Healing with gem elixirs or tinctures partly uses the science of color healing and partly uses the science of gem power. Gem elixirs are easy to make and can be an important part of a healer's weapons against disease.

A. K. Bhattacharya successfully treated patients for years in India with gem elixirs. In his practice he used the seven principal gems given in ancient Sanskrit writings plus three other gems. The seven gems are said to match the seven cosmic rays, light rays that make up the universe. The Kurma Purana of the Hindus says that even the seven planets known to the ancients are condensations of these seven rays of light. These seven rays also match the colors of the seven major chakras in the astral body.

The best gems are authentic, with synthetic gems, man-made to weigh and refract light in the same way as genuine gemstones, next in value. Do not use simulated or glass look-alikes. When creating gem elixirs, choose stones of the purest color, not mixed with any other stone or colors. Ideally, the stone should be tumbled or faceted and have no particles that might come loose in the liquid. Jewels set in silver or gold mountings can be used if they are clean. In Hindu gem therapy, gems are not chosen for the color seen by the physical eye, but by the color seen through a prism or microscope.

A complete list of stones and their uses for diseases follows the procedures for preparing gem elixirs. Pearl and coral are in this list of Hindu healing stones, although technically they are not true stones. Also, it is not necessary to have large gem-stones to make elixirs. A small tumbled or faceted stone of good color works well and is easily inserted and removed from the bottles.

There are two kinds of cat's eye stones. The chrysoberyl cat's eye is extremely expensive; a small cabochon the diameter of the tip of your little finger can cost as much as $7,000. The quartz cat's eye, or crocidolite, is far less expensive and, in my experience, works just as well as the chrysoberyl cat's eye.

The Hindus add to their list of single gem elixirs what are known as Seven-Gem Elixir and Nine-Gem Elixir. The Seven-Gem Elixir uses emerald, diamond, ruby, sapphire, topaz or moonstone, cat's eye, and pearl. The Nine-Gem Elixir adds coral and onyx to the Seven-Gem Elixir.

The gems used to make elixirs will readily discharge their power into water or alcohol. However, the pearl should never be placed in alcohol; alcohol will damage it.

To prepare elixirs for a vast array of diseases, you need at least nine of the gems in the above list, several one- or two-ounce glass bottles with screw caps (preferably bottles colored blue or green), and vodka or pure water. Pure water is best, as it doesn't react adversely with any gemstone. You can use vodka, if you wish, but it isn't necessary. Not only will alcohol damage some stones, but some patients may have negative re-

Making gem elixirs

actions to alcohol in a gem elixir. Never use medicinal or rubbing alcohol.

First, wash and sterilize the bottles. Fill a bottle with water, then drop in the required gem. Seal the bottle with the cap and store in a dark place for seven days and nights. The best time to begin this is after the new moon so you are finished by the next full moon. At the end of this time, shake the bottle gently, and then transfer the liquid into another labeled bottle. The water will not look any different after it is made into gem elixir. Store out of the sunlight.

Wash the gemstone thoroughly and store until you need it again. Always give your stones time to rest between making batches of elixir. A small stone is capable of charging an ounce of water at a time.

The Seven-Gem Elixir is made by placing all seven gems in the bottle at one time. With the Nine-Gem Elixir, place the nine gemstones in the bottle. The rest of the procedure is the same as for a single gem elixir.

Unless patients are very ill, have them take six to twelve drops of the elixir, three or four times a day. For all single gem elixirs, give the more seriously ill patient four to six doses each day. Nine-Gem Elixir is stronger and is only given once or twice a day. The Seven-Gem Elixir is given only two or three times a day. In all chronic cases, one dose per day of Seven- or Nine-Gem Elixir is useful, along with single gem elixirs. It takes time to see any tangible results. (The elixirs may also be added to bath water or massage oils.)

Use the following list of gemstones to determine which ones to give a patient. Sometimes more than one stone will be useful in treating a disease.

Agate, brown: excessive menstrual bleeding, fever, epilepsy, water retention
Amber: colds, ulcers, malignant and benign growths, soreness, hay fever, asthma, goiter, and respiratory diseases
Amethyst: gout, nightmares, eye diseases.
Carnelian or bloodstone: hemorrhages, ulcers
Cat's Eye: skin diseases, acne, headaches, indigestion, cancer, paralysis, uterine diseases
Coral: liver diseases, impure blood, high blood pressure, skin

ailments, hemorrhoids, sexual diseases, gallstones, hemorrhoids, hepatitis, liver trouble

Diamond: gastritis, problems of the heart and circulatory system, eye diseases, various forms of paralysis, enlarged
spleen, epilepsy, diabetes, infected glands, itchy skin,
menopause, nephritis, sterility

Emerald: insomnia, throbbing, tension, headache pain, weak digestion, colic, cancer, skin problems, hypertension, heart
trouble, ulcers, colitis, diarrhea, duodenal ulcer, gastric
ulcer, gastritis, heartburn, indigestion, vomiting

Garnet: eczema, psoriasis, skin eruptions

Hematite: eye diseases, hemorrhages of the lungs or uterus, sun-
stroke, headache

Jade: heart palpitations, difficult childbirth

Lapis lazuli: prevent miscarriage

Moonstone: fever, epilepsy, mental illness

Onyx: bacterial or virus infections, hyperacidity, insomnia,
brain disorders, glandular diseases

Opal: clears the brain and revives the memory

Pearl: mental problems, diabetes, asthma, gallstones, diarrhea,
menopausal difficulties, Bright's disease, bronchitis, edema,
fevers, persistent low fever, hemorrhages, high blood pressure, influenza, insomnia, kidney stones, melancholia,

pneumonia, rhinitis, tonsillitis, urinary tract disease. Never soak pearls in alcohol. Use only pure water.

Quartz crystal, clear: glandular swellings, glaucoma, conjunctivitis, fevers, abdominal pains, strengthening the heart

Ruby: benefits the liver, spleen, gallbladder, and pancreas. Helps with heart diseases, circulatory problems, anemia, loss of vitality, eye diseases, arthritis, circulatory system, constipation, irregular heartbeat, low blood pressure, heart palpitations, rheumatism, and various mental disturbances

Sapphire: backache, eczema, headache, heart trouble, laryngitis, migraines, neuralgia, neuritis, pericarditis, psoriasis, vertigo

Turquoise: weak eyesight, inflammation of the eyes, headaches, fever, problems with urine retention

Topaz: female problems, colds, lung conditions, sinus and nose problems, throat diseases, asthma, insomnia, epilepsy, laryngitis, childhood infectious diseases, shock, coughs, swollen glands, obesity, pancreas problems

Seven or Nine Gems: Anemia, arthritis, asthma, backache, Bright's disease, bronchitis, cancer, constipation, diabetes, duodenal ulcer, eczema, gallstones, gastric ulcer, swollen glands, heart trouble, irregular heartbeat, hemorrhages, high and low blood pressure, hepatitis, insomnia, kidney stones, liver trouble, melancholia, menopause, nephritis, obesity, heart palpitations, pancreas trouble, pericarditis, pneumonia, psoriasis, rheumatism, sterility, tonsillitis, vomiting

You should be open to using a variety of treatments in your efforts to promote healing in a patient. However, make certain the patient will accept the technique before using it. Some people will not be open to color light therapy or gemstone elixirs.

CHAPTER NINE

Absent Healing

Absent or distant healing is a mental and spiritual process a healer uses when working with patients who aren't present. It is accomplished through mental imagery and an altered state of consciousness, much like the work of shamans. A photo is helpful but isn't necessary. All a healer needs is a name, what town the patient lives in, and a general description of the disease. After much practice, some healers don't even need to know the illness. They can determine this by making contact with the patient's etheric body. Absent or distant healing takes place when a healer contacts the subconscious mind of a patient and sends visualized symbols or pictures that influence the patient's mind to heal the body.

This type of healing will use the Otherworld healing temple built during the meditation in chapter 5. Enter a meditative state, direct your thoughts toward your temple, and you will be there. Then you can call the patient by name. The etheric body of that person will appear in your temple for healing. All of your study on the aura and chakras, meditation, and building your Otherworld healing temple will now bear fruit.

Most doctors will admit that patients are primarily responsible for healing themselves. Patients can't pray and then do nothing else, expecting a healing to fall into their laps. Patients can participate in the healing by using every alternative non-invasive method in this book that seems to work.

By entering an altered state of consciousness in your Otherworld healing temple, you contact the patient, see the disease or damage, and sometimes its cause. Then you trigger a healing through imaged treatment. Some healers may see a patient through a type of X-ray vision, especially when working on broken bones. This type of vision work rarely comes without a lot of practice by a healer, and never by trying to force it. Just relax and let your intuition guide you.

The healer must concentrate on the patient at all times during the healing and not think about the healing itself. Don't dwell on the healing after it is finished because that will siphon off healing energy.

The healer must use mental pictures to convince the patient's subconscious mind to heal the body. The subconscious mind is able to do wonderful things, most of them considered impossible by the conscious mind. The subconscious mind regulates all the body activities, so healing a disease is a relatively insignificant task. Mental pictures will show the patient's subconscious mind how to correct the problem, thus opening up a connection with universal healing energy.

Guided imagery in meditation or absent healing is important in the healing arts. Imagery can increase the natural killer cell activity, increase the production of immunoglobulin, and increase the activity and numbers of disease-fighting lymphocytes.

A good book on anatomy can be helpful. In this way, the healer gets a better idea of where internal organs are.

Understanding the endocrine glands is another vital part of healing. If these are working properly, many illnesses will correct themselves. To understand better how these glands work, a brief description of each follows.

The pituitary gland is in the center of the head, in back of and between the eyes, at the root of the nose. It hangs from the hypothalamus gland, which is attached to the brain. The pituitary gland is really the master gland and controls all the endocrine glands in the body.

The hypothalamus gland is about the size of a sugar cube and is located in the brain. It connects the chemical and neural systems. The thalamus gland is slightly above and to the rear of the hypothalamus. It is the reception area for touch, pain, heat, cold, and muscle sensations.

The pineal gland is behind the thalamus and lies almost in the center of the head. It is only about a half-inch long and it's believed to stimulate the action of the other glands.

The thyroid gland is butterfly-shaped and lies on each side of the throat just above the points of the collarbone. It controls metabolism and the calcium content of the blood. The button-like parathyroid glands are imbedded in the thyroid, two on each side. They help to control blood calcium and the phosphate in the kidneys and pancreas.

The thymus gland lies in the front of the chest and just below the thyroid gland. It governs the actions of the lymph glands for fighting infection.

One adrenal gland sits atop each kidney. These glands produce adrenalin for the sympathetic nervous system. They also release other hormones to regulate the amount of salt and water in the body.

Absent healers work with images and send certain colors of healing energy during an absent healing treatment. In general, red healing energy produces energy for physical body maintenance; it is a stimulus that speeds up sluggish organs. Green energy aids the subconscious mind in replacing or rebuilding damaged areas. Blue energy will support the interaction of body functions, calm pain, relax the body, and soothe the nervous system. Pink energy calms intense nervous conditions. Use white energy for general healing, disinfecting, energizing, stimulating, and normalizing any physical problem.

There are a number of ways to interpret diseases that appear during a healing, but you must find the one that helps you the most. Images of diseases usually appear as symbolic impressions. For example, if you are working on a patient with diabetes, this disease may appear to you as a pipe with a thick, syrupy, reddish brown liquid flowing through it or as large white specks in the blood stream. The white specks could be interpreted as sugar crystals, just as the thick, syrupy liquid would be the blood stream clogged with sugar particles. Broken bones often look like snapped sticks. Painful muscles may appear as long red streaks giving off a fiery heat. Arthritic joints might look like ball bearings coated with pebbles and sand. With practice, you will understand what your intuition is trying to explain.

Several general visualization techniques work well for all healers. These are symbolic techniques only and have nothing to do with physical reality. The subconscious mind deals only with symbols and must be presented with such to understand what you want it to do. If your instincts come up with symbolic techniques other than the ones in this book, use them.

One important fact to remember in all absent, imaged healing is that you must destroy all removed and infected tissue in a psychic, spiritual fire. You might wish to install a large bowl or cauldron in your Otherworld healing temple for this purpose.

Use skin tape to fix cuts and tears in the skin. Clean out clogged blood vessels with a long wire brush. Zap tumors, growths, or cancer cells with a laser light. Cover wounds and bruises with skin putty. Drain poisons from kidneys with a suction faucet. Pick out gallstones and kidney stones with long tweezers, then fill the space with blue healing putty. Lessen pain by saturating the painful area or the entire body with green, blue, or white pain-removal light. Place blue or green ice packs on swollen injuries. Use sandpaper, fine files, or a small grinder to smooth off rough arthritic joints. For broken bones, zap the break with healing light, then tape it together with bone tape, and pack it with bone putty. Or you can use psychic glue for broken bones, torn muscles, and a number of other problems. Tie together a torn muscle or ligament with elastic tape. Stop bleeding by cauterizing the cut with a healing laser. Cover scrapes or sores with large pieces of new skin tape. Use a small suction machine and hose to remove tiny pieces of glass, splinters, bone fragments, small growths, or poisonous crystals in the blood that can become arthritis or other diseases. Let your subconscious mind come up with new ideas that fit your needs.

Paint blue healing gel on painful joints or the entire body to remove pain. Inject lubricating oil into stiff joints. Remove any red threads from the body as these symbolize lines of pain. Do the same with any black threads that may be disease tendrils. Destroy these threads or any removed material in your cauldron of universal flames.

Use sponges to soak up fluid in the lungs, throat, and sinuses. For the hard-to-reach sinuses in the forehead, use a small suction machine.

Infections are carried by the blood, once they establish a hold in body tissues. When this occurs, install a mental germicidal filter in the blood stream to trap and kill all germs and foreign matter.

The only way to explain how to do absent healing through correct visualization is to give examples. Then you can explore further on your own, discovering what symbols and impressions work. Stories from my healing classes illustrate the many valuable uses of visualization used in healing.

In one session, we worked on Al, a diabetic. Al had let his diet and medication slide until he was in serious difficulties. We mentally installed filters in several of the main arteries to filter out the sugar crystals. Then we washed out the liver and pancreas in a green healing solution to dissolve any harmful residue. After checking for any viral infection that might be lurking undetected, we reset the pituitary, pineal, and adrenal glands so that they properly controlled the insulin. We finished by bathing the patient in blue and green healing lights. Al's blood levels evened out, and by following his diet and medication schedule as he should, he was soon able to dispense with insulin shots.

Leukemia is an insidious and potentially deadly disease. When Jim requested a healing, he was in the middle stage of the disease. We began by injecting blue healing energy into the long bones of his legs and arms, and into the pelvic bone, to normalize the production of white blood cells. Then we sent streams of red energy into those same areas to increase the production of red blood cells. We injected green energy into the liver, spleen, and lymph glands to destroy any remaining cancer cells, and finished by bathing his body in white and gold light. Jim improved greatly but refused to return for another healing treatment, believing that one session should do it. One healing session is never enough for any disease. Jim's disease eventually gained ground again.

When treating a respiratory infection, first you need to get rid of the congestion. Soak it up with sponges or install a suction faucet. Then eliminate the cause of the inflammation. You may need to spray germicidal spray through the lungs and sinuses.

In pneumonia, you need to remove as much of the lung fluid as you can. Next, pour blue gel into the lungs to remove pain. Finish by filling both lungs with white healing light. You may need to also install germicidal filters in the bloodstream to help remove viruses and bacteria.

For asthma, check the lungs, nose, sinuses, throat, and bronchial tubes for infection and irritation. Drain off any accumulated fluid, and spray these areas with blue liquid to minimize any further irritation.

In dealing with emphysema, you will notice that the lungs will look distended and stiff, with the inside walls dry and likely covered in what looks like blisters. Using your Otherworld tweezers, remove the blisters and any damaged air sacs. Disinfect the lungs with blue or green light. Fill any holes left by removal of tissue with body putty. Then flood the lungs with a softening healing oil that will give them elasticity. Finish by flooding the entire chest area with gentle white light.

Frequently children suffer painful earaches, although adults may get them on occasion. First drain off the infection in the inner ear. Check the eustachian tubes; if they are blocked, gently run a small, long brush through to open them. Then flood the entire ear and the tube with soothing blue gel to re-move the pain.

When working on head colds and sinus infections, drain off the infection, making sure that you get into all the sinus cavities. Open any blockages. Spray all the infected areas with blue healing liquid to kill the germs and flood the head with white light.

A patient with a sore throat will often have several con-nected areas infected at the same time. Check the throat, si-nuses, and lungs. Suction out any infection and open any blockages. Paint the infected areas with green healing gel. In-stall a germicidal filter in the blood stream and inject a univer-sal antibiotic.

Skin problems such as rashes, moles, or warts can be treated in a similar way. First check the blood for impurities and install a germicidal filter to handle that problem. Spray a disinfectant over the diseased area. Paint a violet-colored skin peeler on the affected skin and then peel off the mole, wart, or rash. Recover the area with new skin tape.

When dealing with a breast tumor or cancer, check for any tiny black threads issuing from the main site. Remove these and burn them. Check the lymph glands for contamination. Shrink the tumor with a violet laser light and remove any re-maining portion with the tweezers. Install filters in the lymph glands to catch any floating cancer cells and destroy them. Flood the entire body with brilliant white healing light.

When healing internal growths or tumors, be certain to remove all the immediately surrounding tissue and blood vessels when you remove the tumor or growth itself. Burn these. Pack green gel into the site of removal and hold it in place with body tape. Flood the entire area with blue light to remove the pain, followed by white light for healing.

When working to eradicate any cancer or tumor, always make certain you destroy any removed tissue in your cauldron of spiritual fire. You don't want the vibrations of such deadly diseases floating around in the atmosphere.

Cancer requires long-term healing sessions. Use the above-mentioned healing techniques, and expand upon them as necessary. You may need to install cancer-killing filters in the bloodstream if no tumors are found. This ensures that any floating malignant cells are trapped and destroyed.

Chronic or recurring headaches can be debilitating and frequently involve more than blood vessels. Check first for any aneurysms; if you find one, reinforce it with flexible body tape. If there are no aneurysms, check that the pituitary, pineal, thalamus, hypothalamus, thyroid, and thymus glands are working properly. Reset them if necessary. The endocrine glands are reset by visualizing them with a dial with settings for low, medium, and high. You will then be able to see if the gland is working overtime (high) or not enough (low). Set the dial at medium for proper operating. Find any expanded or contracted blood vessels (usually at the base of the skull and in the neck). If expanded, cool them with blue gel packs. If contracted, pack them with red gel packs until they expand to the proper size. Bathe the entire head in blue and white light to ease the pain and tension.

Nervous headaches are usually caused by nervous tension and a depletion of energy. Send red energy into the nervous system to recharge the body's energy. Bathe the entire body in blue gel to relieve tension and pain. Finish by shooting gold light throughout all the aura levels. Since nervous headaches frequently cause the shoulder muscles to tighten, you will need to massage blue gel into these areas to relieve the pain and loosen the tension.

Heart and artery problems require a slightly different approach because you must stop time while working on these. This does not harm the patient or stop the heart. Picture a clock beside the patient and order it to stop. Check out the entire heart—valves, muscles, and arteries. Replace any bad valves by picking out the old ones and installing new ones. Inject red energy into damaged muscles. Clean out any clogged arteries with a long brush. Flood the entire chest with blue light to relieve pain and then gold light to continue healing indefinitely. Return to the clock and order it to resume time.

When working with the liver and gallbladder, remove any stones or growths; fill the cavities with body putty. Wash out the organs with a green liquid and drain off this waste. Spray the inside with blue energy until the liver or gallbladder attains a healthy color. Flood the entire area with blue light to relieve pain. If the patient has cirrhosis or hepatitis, the cleaning may take some time. Be certain that you drain off all the waste you wash from the liver. Raise the body's healing rate by 25 percent. You can do this by again visualizing a dial set in the organ involved. The face of the dial will be marked in easy-to-read degrees. Simply set the dial 25 percent higher than it was.

For kidney or bladder infections, examine the complete urinary tract for areas of infection and spray it with green liquid to kill gems. Wash the entire tract with green germicide and drain off the waste. Remove any stones or growths. Flush the entire system with blue energy to relieve pain.

Intestinal and stomach ulcers need immediate pain relief, so flood the entire intestinal tract from one end to the other with blue energy for pain. Using a green laser light, destroy the ulcer. Fill the cavity with blue body putty and seal with body tape. Coat the entire intestinal tract and stomach, inside and out, with white healing paint. Finish by installing a germi-cidal filter in the blood stream, as many ulcers are caused by a bacteria.

When healing the spinal column for whatever reason, check it from top to bottom for broken or chipped vertebrae, herniated disks, and bone spurs. Put broken or chipped verte-brae back together with bone glue and patch with bone putty. Grind off any bone spurs. Be sure to check the inside of the vertebrae for spurs often lurk on the inside. Pack blue gel around herniated disks to shrink them and cushion between the vertebrae. Bathe the entire spine, nerves, and adjacent muscles with blue healing light to relieve pain.

This type of healing imagery can be used whenever you are in meditation, even if the patient lives near you. Sometimes the subconscious mind will be more open to symbolic images if the patient is asleep while you are working.

CHAPTER TEN

Healing Images

The use of a poppet in healing is known as sympathetic magic, meaning that the healer performs a healing ceremony with a created image in an effort to affect the patient's subconscious mind. As in absent healing, the magic follows the thought to the patient whom you have in mind and produces the results. This magical art can be misused, as when making dolls to harm another person, but that was never its primary use. No healer will indulge in negative magic.

Sympathetic magic has a long history in the healing arts of the ancient cultures. For example, in ancient Egypt, physicians made images out of wax or clay and red substances to symbolize blood. They then added a great variety of minerals and plants to these images, all in an effort to persuade the patient's subconscious mind to help with the healing.

In 1869, J. E. Quibell excavated several sites in Egypt. One of these was the house of a medical magician who lived at

Thebes. In the ruins of this house he found four small wax figures that represented the sons of Horus,[1] two clay *ushabtis* (or *shawabtis*),[2] and a wooden box with an image of the goddess Isis, mistress of magic, on the lid. This box contained a number of small magical papyrus scrolls. However, the scrolls were so delicate that they could not be completely unrolled. The box also contained four ivory curved wands with mythical creatures painted on them. These magical wands were used for making gestures when the magician made such items as talismans and amulets. Also inside were small human figures (poppets) made of clay, red and black inks, reed pens, and stone beads and amulets.

Today these little human-shaped images can be made of cloth, wood, clay, or, in an emergency, even paper. Each one is made to represent a specific person. The power doesn't lie within the poppet, but within the will and intent of the healer-magician.

A poppet usually looks something like a gingerbread cookie. It does not have to be very large, just big enough to hold some herbs and perhaps a stone or two. You don't have to be a seamstress or even handy with a needle to make a poppet. In fact, you can use fabric glue to hold the two pieces of cloth together.

The supplies you will need are few: a small amount of light blue, light green, or white material; fabric glue or thread; a black pen; a small amount of herbs; whatever stones you choose; a long piece of white yarn; two light blue or light green candles; a red candle; sticks or cones of frankincense; and a small basket or box lined with a piece of white material. If you have white material on hand, you can use that to make the poppet instead of colored material. Choose your herbs and stones from the lists later in this chapter.

Tradition holds that something belonging to the person whom the poppet represents should be put inside it, even if this is only a piece of paper with their handwriting. However, you can make a useful poppet without this.

The poppet is best made out of cloth instead of other substances so that you can draw on features that represent the man or woman for whom it is being made. It is also useful to write the person's name across the body of the doll. This enables you to know which doll represents what person, especially if you are working on more than one patient at a time. If you know the patient's sun sign, draw that astrological symbol on the poppet also.

Enlarge the pattern in the following illustration to the size you want. While you are cutting out two pieces of the material for each poppet, visualize the sick person whom you wish to

Poppet image

help by making the healing doll. It is best to finish one poppet before you start on another. You can use either fabric glue (available in fabric shops) to attach the two pieces of material together, or you can sew the pieces together about one-quarter of an inch from the edges. Leave an opening along one side of the poppet. You will use this opening to stuff the doll with herbs and stones. When the poppet is completely stuffed, sew or glue this opening shut.

When choosing the herbs, be sure to include herbs for body, mind, and spirit, as well as for healing. You want to bring the patient back to a balanced life, for healing will not last without balance in all areas and on all levels.

You can also put in certain small gemstones. Try to put one gemstone in the diseased area. You can also include other small stones that will aid in healing.

If the patient has any wounds or visible marks from an illness, draw these onto the poppet in the proper places. During your healing ceremony, cover these marks with wax dripped from a red candle. This symbolizes the healing that will occur in the patient.

After making the outer portion of the poppet, lay it in a basket or small box lined with white cloth. You will finish the healing doll at the full moon. Check an astrological calendar for the correct date, as some ordinary calendars are off by a day.

Have all your needed materials on hand when you begin the final part of assembling the poppet. For the best results, a poppet should be cleansed and empowered on a full moon. You will work on the poppet from one full moon until the next.

At the full moon, place the poppet between two blue or green candles on your altar. Light the candles and burn frankincense incense.

Have your chosen herbs ready. You should use at least three or five different herbs in each poppet. Three and five are magical numbers and are important in spells of all kinds. You do not need to have an even amount of each herb. If you don't have enough herbs on hand to completely fill the poppet, stuff it with cotton batting, leaving enough space for the herbs. The herbs should be dried, not fresh, which may mildew.

Choose your herbs from the following list or consult books on magical herbalism to make correct choices.

Allspice: good health, happiness, banishing negativity, spiritual wisdom

Basil: healing, banishing fear, calming

Bay leaves: good health, reducing stress, spiritual blessings

Carnation petals: healing, success, peace

Chamomile flowers: good health, calmness, peace

Cinnamon: healing, confidence, grounding

Gardenia petals: good health, confidence, happiness, cleansing of the spirit

Juniper berries: healing, happiness, spiritual blessings

Lavender flowers: good health, calmness, banishing negativity

Mugwort: good health, healing of the mind and emotions, connecting with spiritual teachers

Peppermint: healing, eliminating anger, connecting with spiritual teachers

Pine needles: grounding, calming the mind, banishing negativity, reducing stress

Rose petals: good health, eliminating anger, spiritual blessings

Rosemary: grounding, pain relief, banishing negativity, spiritual cleansing

Verbena or vervain: good health, reducing stress, peace, connecting with spiritual teachers

Yarrow flowers: healing, gaining confidence, cleansing the environment

Before stuffing the herbs into the poppet, you must empower them. Place the chosen herbs in a small bowl. Hold the bowl in one hand, while placing your power hand over the herbs. Visualize healing energy pouring into the herbs. Say an incantation, such as this:

> *I bless these herbs with healing power, to heal the body, mind, and soul, of (patient's name) in this hour, that she/he may once again be whole.*

Stuff the herbs carefully into the poppet.

Choose your stone or stones from the following list or consult a good book on magical uses of stones.

General stones for health and healing can be any green, blue, or pink stone. Or you may choose from the following stones.

Agate, moss: a powerful rapid healer

Amber: heals chest problems and digestive diseases, will cleanse the entire system

Amethyst: calms mental problems, purifies the blood, strengthens the immune system, balances all chakras

Aventurine: strong healing powers through the pituitary gland

Bloodstone: cleanses the blood, detoxifies the body

Carnelian: helps regenerate tissue, cleanses the blood, shrinks tumors

Garnet: purifies and regenerates all body systems

Jade: purifies the blood, strengthens the immune system, calms

Lapis lazuli: a great healer and purifier

Malachite: regenerates tissue, strengthens the heart

Moonstone: unblocks the lymphatic system, reduces swelling

Quartz crystal, clear: an extremely powerful all-purpose healer

Quartz, rose: heals mental, emotional, and spiritual distresses

Tourmaline, watermelon: soothes the nervous system and the aura field

Turquoise: a master healer, strengthens and regenerates the entire body

If you can't afford to buy a variety of stones, you can use clear quartz crystal alone. However, it is more effective to have more than one kind of stone.

Hold your chosen stones in one hand with your power hand over them. Empower them by saying:

O, stones of star and earth and sea, heal (patient's name).
So must it be.

Place the stones inside the poppet. If you have a personal object from the patient, put that inside also. Sew or glue the poppet closed.

Take up your red candle and dribble wax over any wounds, cuts, or blemishes you have drawn onto the poppet. While you do this, say:

Red as the blood of life, I mark the wounds of (patient's name).
I seal them. I bind them. I heal them.

Tie a long piece of white yarn around the middle of the poppet to symbolize the doll's connection with spirit and with the patient. Leave one long end hanging loose. Say:

This cord connects (patient's name) and this healing doll. When the healing is complete, at my word the tie will be broken.

Snuff out the candles and return the poppet to the basket.

Every day, light the candles and incense, and say the following chant while holding the poppet in both hands. Do this until the next full moon. Concentrate on the patient being totally well while saying the chant. This builds a psychic link with the patient. You can also pray however you wish.

Chant three times:

(Patient's name) is restored and whole. This is my wish; this is
my goal. Disease, be gone! All illness flee! This is my will.
So mote it be.

Each time you finish the ritual, place the poppet back into the basket or box and cover it with the white cloth.

Tradition says that a poppet should never be destroyed but given to the person it represents. However, this is not always a good idea, as most people connect poppets with voodoo dolls and would be shocked to know a healer made a doll of them. That is why each poppet should have a white thread or piece of yarn tied around its waist with one long end of the thread hanging loose. When the poppet has done its work and needs to be dismantled, the healer-magician should hold the doll and chant:

The tie between (patient's name) and this doll is now broken.
All healing energy left within this doll flies to (patient's name).
Only good shall come of this action.

Then the white yarn is cut free, the poppet opened, and the herbs sprinkled on the earth. Any personal object from the sick person that was enclosed in the poppet is buried in the earth. Any gemstones that were included can be cleansed and reused. The remaining parts of the poppet can then be safely burned or buried.

Never save a poppet to use again. That is tantamount to saying you don't believe in your healing work. If a patient does become ill a second time, make a new poppet.

1. The four sons of Horus were used to represent the four directions during magical rituals. Modern magicians frequently use four different-colored candles to represent these directions.
2. Because Egyptian hieroglyphs didn't include vowels as we know them, there are several possible spellings for ancient Egyptian words.

CHAPTER ELEVEN

Talismans and Amulets

From the beginning of civilization, people have worn or carried amulets and talismans to which they attributed certain powers. Amulets are some of the most common objects found in archaeological sites. They date back to prehistoric times and are not confined to any one place or historical period or culture.

The modern equivalents of these ancient magical objects are rosaries, saints' medals, crosses, crystal pendants, a rabbit's foot, a lucky coin, the Egyptian ankh, and the charm bracelet. In the Punjab area of India, people wear copper bracelets, rings, and earrings to protect against arthritis and sciatica. In Oriental cultures, jade bracelets and anklets symbolize protection against misfortune.

The dictionary defines an amulet as "a charm often inscribed with a magical incantation or symbol to protect and aid the wearer." Talisman means "a charm to avert evil and bring good fortune."

Ordinarily, amulets are naturally formed substances like herbs, stones, or animal claws. They are chosen for their unusual forms or colors. Some, however, are man-made representations of these objects. People believe they will safeguard the owner from trouble and attract happiness and good luck. A natural amulet is said to be full of universal and earth energy, while the man-made amulet is empowered by magic or faith.

Some believe that the word *amulet* is derived from an Arabic root, which means "to bear, to carry." Others hold that the word is derived from the Latin *amuletum*, which is an object that protects a person from trouble.

The ancient Egyptians had several names for amulet. One early Egyptian name for amulet was *bekau*, which is a form of the word for magic. Another was *udjaou*; the literal translation is "the thing that keeps safe." Other times the word *mekti*, or "protector," was used.

Talismans are similar to amulets, except that a talisman is a man-made object and is charged through ritual to do one specific duty for a specific person, while amulets are general in nature. Talisman is derived from the Greek root *teleo*, which means, "to consecrate."

Charms can be symbols or written words and combine the functions of both talismans and amulets. The modern charm bracelet is very old in origin. Examples of charm bracelets and anklets have been found in early Roman ruins.

Amulets were very popular among the Egyptians and were frequently part of the grave goods in tombs, where they were inserted into the mummy wrappings. Most amulets had small holes in them so that they could be hung on a neck chain, pectoral, or bracelet (like the modern charm bracelets), or fastened to a ring. A pectoral is a wide collarlike piece of Egyptian jewelry that laid flat around the neck and hung down onto the chest.

Amulets were made according to strict magical rules and traditions. It is possible that certain priests oversaw their production. An ancient document known as the MacGregor Papyrus listed seventy-five different amulets, the names by which they were known, and their uses. This information is verified by a list carved on the walls of the temple at Dendera. This list gives the materials from which the amulets should be made. The ancient Egyptians used amulets in specific shapes for certain results. The following figure illustrates a few of the talismans and amulets with which you may not be familiar. Today, most people are familiar with certain reproductions of ancient Egyptian amulets.

Although Egyptian amulets were made of every known material, the finest ones were carved out of stone, such as lapis

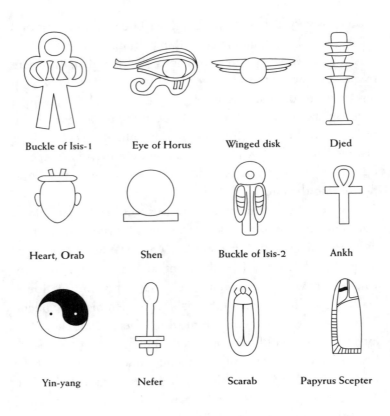

Buckle of Isis-1 Eye of Horus Winged disk Djed

Heart, Orab Shen Buckle of Isis-2 Ankh

Yin-yang Nefer Scarab Papyrus Scepter

Various talismans and amulets

lazuli, carnelian, turquoise, feldspar, serpentine, and steatite. Sometimes metals such as gold, copper, bronze, and iron were used. However, the largest number of amulets found in excavations were made of faience. Faience is a paste made out of ground quartz crystal, molded, covered with an opaque colored glaze, and then fired. Today, copies of Egyptian amulets are frequently made of clay, ceramic, or silver.

In this chapter I will use the *amulet* to describe all of these magical objects, whether they are amulets, talismans, or charms.

There are actually two kinds of amulets. One type is inscribed with magical words, and the other type is not. For example, Egyptian amulets such as the scarab were inscribed on the reverse side of the amulet, while those made by medieval ceremonial magicians often consisted only of magical words engraved on metal or written on paper.

You can make many of the amulets out of clay, thin wood, thin pieces of metal, or draw them out on paper. (See opposite illustration.) Paper amulets are usually carried in a small cloth or leather bag. Each amulet is activated by chanting prayers or certain words over it. You can do the blessing yourself. If you purchase an amulet, you still need to activate it by chanting.

Amulets can be a valuable healing tool, for the visible images work on the patient's subconscious mind and reinforce any other healing methods you are using.

A typical ritual for activating the powers within an amulet is simple to do with a minimum of material. Light two white candles and lay the amulet between them. Light frankincense incense. Fill a small bowl with a little water and place a pinch of salt on a saucer. Hold the amulet in one hand, with your power hand over it.

Chant: "Fire, Water, Earth, and Air, I call upon your powers fair. Empower this amulet for me. For so I will. So shall it be."

If you make this amulet for another person, be certain to state, "I bless this amulet for (patient's name)" before you do the actual blessing.

Quickly pass the amulet in the heat above the candle flames, then through the incense smoke. Sprinkle a few grains of salt on the amulet; dip the salt back onto the saucer. Sprinkle a few drops of water onto the amulet from the bowl. The amulet is now ready to wear.

The following list of amulets will help you decide which ones a sick person may wish to wear or carry.

Acorn: This represents good luck, protection, and long life. It also symbolizes the accomplishment of a difficult task, usually one that takes time.
Apple: This represents healing and long life.
Ankh: This is also called the looped cross or *crux ansata*. It

meant life or everlasting life. All Egyptian deities are portrayed holding an ankh. It is a very powerful protective symbol and the oldest of Egyptian amulets.

Bats: In the Chinese culture, the image of two bats gave good fortune.

Bells: This amulet frightens away evil.

Birds: The Chinese believed that images of the stork and crane brought good health and long life.

The Buckle of Isis: This amulet is also called the *tjet* or *tjed*. Some writers believe this object represents the buckle on the girdle of the goddess Isis, while others think it represents female genitalia. Also called the knot of Isis, this amulet was always carved out of red stone, such as jasper or carnelian, or other red substances, for the blood of Isis was said to contain great magical powers. On rare occasions, archaeologists have discovered the buckle made of gold or substances covered with gold. It was the all-powerful symbol of the goddess Isis, who was a powerful magician and healer. It is used for protection and the removal of blockages.

Bull: This represents strength and virility.

Butterfly: This represents eternal life and reincarnation, or a transformation within this life.

Cat: This protective amulet was connected with the Egyptian goddess Bast or Bastet, who gave aid to those who called upon her. To the Egyptians, the black cat was an extremely powerful healing symbol.

Clover: The four-leaf clover represents hope, good luck, love, and faith. The typical three-leaf Irish shamrock symbolizes good luck, love, and prosperity. The three-leaf clover was also used as a magical emblem by the Greeks, Romans, and Egyptians, who believed it gave immortality, riches, and protection from evil.

Conch shell: This represents protection against evil.

Cricket: This represents good luck.

Cross: The equal-armed cross is an ancient sun symbol of protection.

Djed: This amulet was connected with the power of the Egyptian god Osiris, and was worn only by the dead to assure stability of the afterlife. Although sometimes this object is said to be a symbol of the tree in which the body of Osiris was hidden, it is more likely that this represents the backbone of the god Osiris. The four crossbars represent the four cardinal directions. In modern terms, the *djed* can be used to give strength to the backbone or spine.

Dog: This amulet is a warning image against evil.

Eagle: This ancient symbol of the sun god gives vitality and strength. The eagle was also considered to be a messenger from the gods to humans.

Elephant: To the Hindus, this emblem represented the elephant-headed god Ganesha, who removed all obstacles and difficulties.

Eye of Horus: The ancient word for this amulet was *utchat* or *udjat*. It symbolized the all-seeing eyes of the god Horus and ensured good health. The eyes of Horus were considered to be the sun and the moon. It was made of silver, gold, hematite, carnelian, or lapis lazuli. The *udjat* can give the wearer good health and physical protection.

Fairy: This represents unexpected help from the Otherworld.

Fish: This image has long been an important symbol used in many cultures. To the Egyptians, it meant abundance, prosperity, happiness, and wealth. To the Hindus, it meant protection, fertility, and wealth. Two fish mean fertility.

Frog: This amulet was associated with the Egyptian goddess Hekat and symbolized fertility, fruitfulness, resurrection, inspiration, and a new life. The Burmese use the frog image for protection, especially for children.

Hand: The Hand of Fatima is an Arabic symbol of protection and good fortune. However, the hand symbol goes back to Stone Age cultures. The Egyptians used the hand as protection against evil arising from envy. The Etruscans used it as a symbol of justice and victory. The image of a life-sized hand guards against evil and brings good luck. It is more powerful if you use the outline of the hand belonging to the person who will receive this amulet.

Heart: This was thought to be the source of the power of life and also the source of individual good or evil. The Egyptian word for heart was *ab*, and the image was always made in a red color. The *ab* brought love, protected against hatred, and symbolized the power of the subconscious mind, vital power, and the seat of the soul.

Holly: This ancient emblem is for good luck, friendship, and goodwill.

Horse, white: This amulet represents long life and determination to gain what you desire.

Horseshoe: This is for good luck and protection from evil.

Ivy: This represents faithful friendship.

Key: This was an ancient symbol in many cultures. It represents knowledge and the opening of doors to the unknown. It was sacred to the Roman deities Apollo and Diana. It was also an emblem of the god Janus and represented prudence, memory of the past, and perception of the future. The Japanese said that three keys brought happiness, riches, and love. In many other countries, three keys represented love, wealth, and good health.

Ladybug: A protection against poverty, this image attracts wealth and is also said to remove illness. The Norse believed that ladybugs came to earth by means of lightning strikes.

Lion's head: This amulet represents strength.

Moon: When a crescent moon, with the horns pointing to the left, is worn, it symbolizes protection against bad luck and the gaining of incoming prosperity.

Monkey: To the Hindus, this emblem represented the god Hanuman, who brought great good fortune.

Nefer: Worn as a pendant on necklaces, this object may be a stylized musical instrument. It was usually made of carnelian, red stone, or red porcelain and worn on necklaces. It represented joy, strength, happiness, and good luck.

Papyrus scepter: The Egyptian word for this image was *uadj*. It was made of light green or blue substances. This amulet represented the power of the goddess Isis over abundant harvest. It also symbolizes vitality, renewed youth, and constant growth.

Pig: This is a symbol of fertility, good fortune, and protection.

Pyramid: A version of the sacred triangle, the pyramid means protection and indicates that helpful knowledge will be discovered.

Rabbit's foot: Hopefully, you will not buy a real one but will settle for a man-made one instead. It represented great good luck and protection.

Scarab: The most popular amulet in ancient Egypt was the scarab, or *kheper*. The use of this amulet predates the pyramids. Connected with the god Kheper, the scarab amulets often had hieroglyphic messages carved on the underside. This image of the dung beetle represents new life, resurrection, strength, immortality, and good luck.

Shen: This Egyptian symbol represents the sun in its orbit and means eternity and long life.

Snake or serpent: This image represents wisdom and drawing power from the earth.

Spider: The Etruscans believed that spider images gave wisdom, foresight, and riches. Other cultures credited the spider with great ancient wisdom, inspiration, and protection.

Stars: This image represents hope and the fulfillment of wishes.

Tortoise: The Chinese used an image of the tortoise for protection against black magic and to attract good health and long life.

Tusk: Usually a boar's tusk, this is a symbol of good fortune, success, and protection.

Unicorn: Many cultures believed in the existence of the unicorn and credited it with the ability to grant good luck, fierceness, purity, and protection.

Winged disk: An ancient symbol of the sun god, this image
   grants the wearer protection from accidents and all serious
   threats to life. The circle portion of the winged disk represents total protection from all evil.
Wishbone: This symbolizes that wishes will be granted.
Yin and yang symbol: Known in the Orient, this is a circle divided
   into a white section (yang) and a black section (yin) by a
   wavy line. It represents perfect balance.

Amulets can be carried in the pocket or purse, hung on
chains as pendants, or several of them worn on a charm
bracelet. They may also be put into in healing boxes, as described in chapter 12.

Another way to use the amulet symbols is to make a healing plaque for a specific person and carve healing symbols
onto that plaque. Write out the patient's name in runes in the
center of the plaque. Writing in another alphabet is more
powerful because it requires more concentration. Or you may
simply draw appropriate runes that represent the qualities you
want to empower in the plaque. Sketch out symbols from the
above list around this name. See the illustration on page 155
for examples of healing plaques.

The following list of Nordic runes will help you write out
the name and also determine what each rune means. This list is

RUNES

ᚠ F	ᚢ U, V	ᚦ Th	ᚨ A	ᚱ R
ᚲ C, K	ᚷ G	ᚹ W	ᚺ H	ᚾ N
ᛁ I	ᛃ J	ᛇ Ei, Y	ᛈ P	ᛉ Z
ᛋ S	ᛏ T	ᛒ B	ᛖ E	ᛗ M
ᛚ L	◇ Ng	ᛞ D	ᛟ O	Triskeleon
Unknown	Battle Ax	World Tree	Sun Wheel	Moon
What's this?				

152

in alphabetical order according to the spelling of the rune. I have chosen the Nordic runes because they are easy to draw or paint.

Ansuz: alphabet letter *A.* transformation, new goals, information that changes your life

Berkano: alphabet letter *B.* new beginnings

Dagaz: alphabet letter *D.* enlightenment

Ehwo: alphabet letter *E.* new attitude, steady progress

Eihwaz: alphabet letter *EI, I, Y.* end of a matter, situation, or problem

Elhaz: alphabet letter *Z.* blockages removed

Fehu: alphabet letter *F.* money, fulfillment, good luck, goals reached

Gebo: alphabet letter *G.* great good fortune

Hagalaz: alphabet letter *H.* delays while waiting for the right time

Ingwaz: alphabet letter *NG.* benefits from family

Isa: alphabet letter *I.* no movement seen

Jera: alphabet letter *J.* no quick results

Kenaz: alphabet letter *C, K.* determination

Laguz: alphabet letter *L.* hidden movement below the surface

Mannaz: alphabet letter *M.* positive link with the gods

Naudhiz: alphabet letter *N.* caution needed to succeed

Othalaz: alphabet letter *O*. inherited genes or property

Perdhro: alphabet letter *P*. unexpected changes

Raidho: alphabet letter *R*. getting to the truth

Sowilo: alphabet letter *S*. time of renewal, advancement of plans

Thurisaz: alphabet letter *TH*. news from a distance, inner strength to pass a time of waiting

Tiwaz: alphabet letter *T*. victory

Uruz: alphabet letter *U, V*. advancement, good fortune, manifestation

Wunjo: alphabet letter *W*. security, comfort, happiness

The last seven symbols on the chart are not actual runes but mystical pictograms used by the Norse. They are powerful when used for magical purposes.

Moon: an orderly change, a transformation

Ship: movement, transforming problems into positive solutions

Sun wheel: inner guidance, seeking spiritual truths and answers

Thor's Hammer: increase, protection, willpower, protection from all negatives

Triskelion: a form of the sun wheel. Movement, advancement of plans

Unknown symbol: wealth, material success, material gain

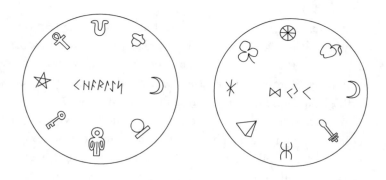

Healing plaques

World Tree: divine guidance, total protection, overpowers all negatives

To make a healing plaque for yourself or another person, use colored clay (that can be air- or oven-dried), and an awl, thin knife, or toothpick for drawing designs on the clay. Work on a flat, smooth surface. Work a ball of clay until it clings together, visualizing good health for the patient. Flatten it into a circle. Roll it smooth with a rolling pin and then cut out the circle with a sharp knife. Etch onto this circle any healing runes you have chosen, plus the name of the person for whom the plaque is made. If the clay can be air-dried, place it in a warm place where it will not be disturbed. If it must be baked, bake the clay on a metal cookie sheet according to directions on the box the clay came in. Baked clay may have a strong odor while in the oven, so you may need to open a window for ventilation. Remove from the oven at the recommended length of time, and cool the clay on the cookie sheet.

The ancient Babylonians used what is called a devil-trap to keep evil out of a house. These devil-traps consisted of a bowl with a magical spell written in spiral fashion, with the beginning of the spell on the outer edge and the ending in the center of the bowl. These bowls were buried under the foundation of a house, or under or near the threshold.

Today, these bowls can be made to trap all negative thoughts, words, and deeds before they enter the house of a sick person.

The bowl or saucer should be fairly flat, as this will make it easier to write upon. Write the following spell in black paint in a spiral fashion on the bowl or saucer. "No evil or negativity may enter this house. It is trapped inside this bowl and returned to the earth for purification." Then bury the bowl near the threshold of the main door if possible. If it isn't possible to bury the bowl, place it under the porch or in the crawl space under the house. If you live in an apartment and have no way to bury the bowl, you can write the spell on a circle of paper and tuck it under the doormat.

CHAPTER TWELVE

Healing Charms and Spells

Healers have made and used healing charms and spells for thousands of years. The original healers were also priest/priestess-magicians who knew that magic, medicine, and religion needed to be combined to heal.

Every ancient culture had deities who specialized in healing. For example, the Sumerians called the god Ea the founder of healing and the patron of herbalists and physicians. They considered that all water had healing properties; therefore, all patients were washed thoroughly. Their god Ninazu was called the Master Physician, and the goddess Ninhursag was also connected with healing.

We know more about the ancient Egyptian culture than many others because of the surviving scrolls and papyri. The Egyptian goddess Sekhmet was the most important of healing deities and was directly associated with medical doctors. However, Isis was also known as the goddess of magic and healing. The gods Horus and Thoth were also associated with the magical healing arts. The physicians, or *wabus*, were priests of these deities and primarily worked in the healing temples, where they treated patients with a combination of medicine, religion, and magic.

Two ancient Egyptian temples were known for miraculous cures. One was the Temple of Dendera, where the physicians used magical water in their cures, followed by magically induced sleep for the patients. The other temple was the mortuary temple of Queen Hatshepsut at Deir el Bahari. The upper terrace of this temple was specifically dedicated to Imhotep and Amenhotep, both of whom were regarded as great physicians.

However, there was another minor branch of physicians, who likely worked among the common people. These were the *sunu*, or lay-physicians, who were not directly attached to a temple. The *sunu* used all the techniques known to the *wabu* priests but used more magic in their healings than their counterparts did. Frequently, they wrote out little protective spells on slips of papyrus that were put into small leather pouches to hang around the neck of a patient.

Ancient Irish medicine included charms and incantations, many of which have survived in folklore and folk medicine. Folk charms can soothe the patient's nerves while acting as a remedial agent.

An example of a folk remedy is four thieves vinegar. During the years of the Black Plague in Europe, a band of thieves came up with a recipe for four thieves vinegar. They swore that this vinegar and herb combination protected them from catching the plague while they plundered the bodies and houses of dead plague victims. The thieves would bathe their hands, arms, necks, and heads with this vinegar. Today we know that vinegar is a type of antiseptic, and some doctors use a vinegar and water spray to disinfect their examination rooms.

To make four thieves vinegar, put a quarter ounce of each of the following herbs into a glass container: calamus root, cinnamon, ground cloves, ground nutmeg, lavender blossoms, mint leaves, thyme, hyssop, rosemary needles, rue, sage, and wormwood. Slice two garlic cloves into the herbs. Add one quart of apple cider vinegar. If you wish, you can heat the vinegar to boiling before adding it to the herbs. Cover the container with a tight lid. Let sit in a warm room for five days. Strain the mixture through a fine sieve or cloth. Add a quarter ounce of powdered camphor if you wish. Then pour into a labeled bottle.

This mixture smells more like a salad dressing than a disinfectant, so you can use it in sick rooms and around the house without offending anyone. In its time, this recipe was considered to be magic, because no one could explain why it worked.

Like many other types of alternative healing and magic, herbal charms and spells aren't instantaneous. Nor will a magical spell work if you only do it one time or with a skeptical attitude. The healer-magician's attitude is very important. Negative thinking has no place in magic. A healer must visualize the patient at all times as healed and free of disease.

There is a standard rule in magic pertaining to the phases of the moon. To decrease anything, work from the day after the full moon until the next new moon; this is called the waning moon. To increase anything, work from the day after the new moon until the next full moon; this is called the waxing moon. Growths and such should be worked on during the waning moon, while wounds and sores should be worked on during the waxing moon. Diseases like pneumonia, lung diseases, and heart problems should be worked on during the waning moon to draw out infection or damage and on the waxing moon to strengthen the organs and muscles.

There are many magical healing recipes, some of which have come down to us in folklore and folk medicine from hundreds of years ago.

Healing oil heals the spirit more than the body. To make healing oil, clean and sterilize a small glass jar, preferably green or blue in color. It must have a tight lid. Some healers will paint the outside of several small jars with translucent paint in the colors they want and save them especially for magical use. Measure out equal portions of rose petals, rosemary leaves, and hyssop, as much as it will take to fill the jar of your choice. Put these into the jar and cover with cold-pressed almond oil. Set the jar where it can get sunlight and moonlight for seven days. Do this beginning on the day after the new moon. At the end of the seven days, strain the herbs and oil through several layers of cheesecloth or through a very fine sieve. Return the oil to the colored jar and cap tightly. Use this oil sparingly to anoint the patient's brow, over the heart chakra, and on the palms of the hands and the soles of the feet.

If you like to use incense that is burned on incense charcoal, you can make your own healing incense. In a mortar and pestle grind together one tablespoon of dried rose petals, one-fourth teaspoon of dried dragon's blood resin, one tablespoon of juniper berries, and one teaspoon of yarrow flowers. Store this mixture in a small sealed jar. Burn a small amount of it on incense charcoal in a censer during healing rituals.

Healing water is similar to Four Thieves Vinegar, although it is primarily used as a psychic cleanser. Do not drink this. It is used to wash the hands before and after a healing. Bring to a boil one pint of pure water—no additives—in a pan. Fluoridated tap water isn't a good choice. Add one teaspoon of saffron, one-half cup of dried rose petals, one-half cup of lavender flowers, and one tablespoon of ground orrisroot. Remove immediately from heat and cover with a tight lid. Let stand three to four minutes. Strain through a fine strainer or cloth. Store in a blue or crystal clear bottle that can be tightly capped.

A healing pillow or small herbal charm bag can be helpful to a sick person. Not only is it a constant reminder that someone cares and is working for their healing, the scents of the herbs can be soothing and relaxing. See chapter 10 for a list of appropriate herbs for healing pillows and bags, and chapter 8 for a list of colors and their magical uses when choosing material colors. A pillow stuffed with mugwort is traditional for dreams. However, if patients are upset by dreams while using sleep pillows, they should discard it.

A healing pillow or small bag to carry doesn't need to be large. It is simply a square of material that is sewn together on three sides, stuffed with the appropriate stones and herbs, and the fourth side sewn shut. See the following illustration for a pattern for a small herbal bag.

Each healing pillow should contain three types of herbs: one for sleep, one for spiritual growth, and one for healing. This little pillow is put under the regular pillow at night. Be

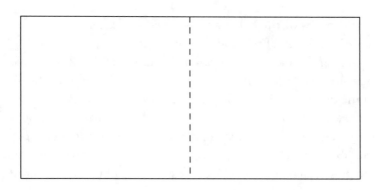

Making an herbal bag

certain that the patient isn't allergic to any of the herbs before you give it to them.

Herb bags are meant to be carried in a pocket or purse, or worn on a cord around the neck like a talisman. An herb bag is sometimes called a sachet. In fact, the idea of sweet-smelling sachets may have originated from herb bags. You may embroider, paint, or draw a symbol on this bag that matches the purpose for which it was made.

Healing pillows and bags should be spiritually cleansed and empowered on a full moon. Consecrate the bag by slowly moving it through the smoke of frankincense incense. Visualize the sick person while saying: "Pure and healing shall you be, O herbs of the earth and sun and sea. Comfort, soothe, and all ills bind, of the body, spirit, mind."

Using the pattern, you can make an herbal bag for the patient to carry. Fold the strip of cloth at the dotted line shown in the diagram. Then sew or glue closed two of the sides, leaving the third side open until you have put in the herbal mixture. A pinch is usually what you can hold between your thumb and forefinger. Mix together a pinch of cinnamon, two pinches of sage, two pinches of rose petals, and two pinches of ground frankincense. Anoint the mixture with three to five drops of sandalwood oil. Put this mixture into the little bag. Sew or glue closed the open side. Give it to the patient to carry at all times. If the patient has lung problems, add two pinches of spearmint leaves to the bag. If the troubles are in the head area or the mind, add two pinches of rosemary. The scent of rosemary is good for headaches.

Other types of healing charms use the powers of the four elements: earth, air, fire, and water. Many of these have come down to us through folklore from many cultures. One of these is healing with air through the power of the wind.

The sick person must do this wind healing. It can only be done for another person if that person is too ill to do it. Collect small fresh leaves, one for each illness you or the person has. Take a dead tree branch with several limbs on it. Go to a place where the wind is strong and push the end of the dead branch into the ground. Push each leaf onto the very tip of a dead branch. Chant "Power of Air, remove all ills. Let (patient's name) be healed and whole." Then leave without looking back. When the wind removes the leaves, the action will release powerful energy for the healing.

Sick people must do most healing charms using the elements themselves. This is part of the patient's involvement and responsibility for healing.

For a charm that uses the power of water, get a small piece of wood that will float, like a Popsicle stick. Write on it every illness you have. Hold it in your hands and visualize your sicknesses going into the stick. Chant: "All illnesses float away from me. This is my will. So shall it be." Place the stick in moving water and let it carry away your illnesses.

Many cultures believe that trees have magical power, particularly in curing illnesses. One only has to visit sacred wells in Ireland and other countries to see that people still believe in this. The shrubs and trees around these wells are frequently decorated with colored strings and ribbons, each denoting a supplicant who wishes to be healed.

Here is one sample of a tree healing. Tie a piece of red thread, string, or yarn loosely around the patient's wrist at bedtime. Leave it on all night. The next morning, take the thread and tie it around a tree or tree branch. Tradition says the illness will pass into the tree and then into the earth, where it will be destroyed.

Another ancient tree healing is simple. Find a tree that you can easily stand against without hitting your head on branches. Circle the tree clockwise nine times, chanting: "Round and round this tree I walk, in search of healing old and deep. O tree of healing, cure my body. Take thou my illnesses and them keep."

Then stand with your back against the trunk and visualize your sickness going into the tree.

Cord or knot magic is another ancient practice. Use a long piece of cord or yarn of natural fibers, if possible. The cord should be green, blue, or white. Assemble small feathers and leaves or twigs of appropriate healing herbs. As you tie nine knots in the cord, chant "Knot one, I tie the sickness tight. Knot two, I bind all mental woes. Knot three, I tie up the sorrows and fears of my emotions. Knot four, I bind all negative thoughts of others and myself. Knot five, I tie all pain and discomfort so it has no power over me. Knot six, I bind all habits, thoughts, or tendencies that may have led to the illness. Knot seven, I tie up healing power that I may draw upon whenever I have need. Knot eight, I bind forgiveness to be freely given to all who harmed me. Knot nine, I bind myself to Divine Spirit, that my mind, body, and spirit may be healed and made whole again." As you tie each knot, insert a feather and a piece of herb into it while you visualize binding up the illness. The following list of feather colors will help you decide which colors to use. The feathers can be found or bought.

When finished, either hang this cord up in the patient's room, or from a tree branch outside.

Black: absorbs all negatives
Black and white: protection
Blue: peace and good health
Brown: health, stability, and grounding
Brown and white: happiness
Gray and white: hope and balance
Orange: energy and success
Pink: love
Purple: deep spirituality
Red: courage, good fortune
White: purification, spirituality, hope, protection, and peace

Another type of healing charm is a spell box. Choose a box that appeals to you and then line it with a color that matches your purpose. The meanings of colors in this instance are:

Black: banishing and absorbing negativity
Blue: healing, peace, and happiness
Gold: great healing energy
Green: healing
Orange: energy
Pink: relaxation
Purple: healing of severe disease and increasing spirituality
Red: maintaining health, strength, and physical energy
Silver: spiritual growth and healing
White: protection, purification, and all purposes
Yellow: confidence

You can also add feathers, stones, and shells to the boxes. You may wish to put a healing poppet in the box to represent the sick person. (See chapter 10).

Shells have special meanings according to their type. Mark clams with a rune so they will be a potent talisman for wearing, carrying, or in the box. (See chapter 11 for rune meanings.) Limpets are for making dramatic positive life changes. Oyster is for good fortune. Sand dollars are for wisdom.

Give the healing box to the ill person and encourage them to add other symbols that have meaning to them. They can open the box whenever they meditate. The symbols will help them connect with spirit and divine healing from the Other-world.

Coriander seeds can be carried in a small bag to prevent illness. Eucalyptus leaves are put into a sleep pillow for colds. Pinecones mean good health, longevity, and fertility; hang them in the house to attract these qualities. Burn thyme to attract good health. Violets can be sprinkled at the corners of the house for healing vibrations and to protect against disease.

There is no end to the possibilities for making healing charms. If you make anything with the desire for healing in your heart, it will attract divine healing energy. The charm's power comes from your positive thoughts and actions, not from any object. The objects are only symbols of those thoughts.

CHAPTER THIRTEEN

Healing Altars

An altar makes any place sacred. Creating an altar opens you to the spiritual dimension of whatever spiritual path you choose. It allows you to express your personal glimpse of the Divine in whatever way you imagine it. Altars are places of centering and rebalancing.

Altars also open a connection between the physical and the spiritual, this world and the Otherworld, which is the source of great healing energy. Healing altars are powerful and valuable in healing the most desperate cases of illness. They are also a way for the family and close friends to participate in healing their loved one.

Altars don't have to be large or elaborate. Begin with what you have. An altar space can be anything: a small shelf, a table, a covered box set in a corner, the top of a dresser, or one corner of a coffee table.

If you wish, place on the altar representations or statues of deities, angels, or saints to symbolize the element of Spirit. Use objects that represent the four elements: a candle for fire; incense for air; a stone or flowers for earth; and a small bowl of water for water. If you plan to light a candle or burn incense on this altar, make certain there is nothing flammable nearby.

For a healing altar, place on it a photo or something that reminds you of the person for whom the altar is being made.

A healing altar attracts people to go there to pray and meditate, to lift their spirits toward the Divine Source. In this way, the family and patient can easily enter an altered state of consciousness, thus aiding any other forms of healing that are being done. These altars bring a state of peace, calmness, and joy that relieves stress in all who sit before them.

If you don't have statues of the deities, angels, or saints for your altar, don't despair. Write the names out carefully on a white card or piece of paper, and place it on the altar. If you want to explore the wide variety of ancient deities and saints before choosing one or more statues, read through the following lists. See the appendix for the list of product suppliers who sell such statues.

ANCIENT HEALING DEITIES

Anu: Ireland. This goddess is associated with health and prosperity.

Anubis: Egypt. Although this god was primarily the deity of death and endings, he also has power over protection, surgery, and hospital stays.

Apollo: Greece. A god of music, Apollo also helps with healing.

Artemis: Greece. This Virgin Huntress goddess has power over mental healing.

Asa: Kenya. Known as the God of Mercy, this deity helps one to survive the impossible or insurmountable.

Bast: Egypt. Shown as a cat-headed goddess, she is associated with healing.

Bel: Ireland. This Sun deity also aids with healing and success.

Brigit/Brighid: Ireland. A goddess of divination, she is also powerful with healing.

Buto: Egypt. This cobra goddess is powerful when called upon for protection.

The Dagda: Ireland. This god was the High King of the Tuatha Dé Danann, and is known for his healing powers.

Diancecht: Ireland. This god was a famous ancient physician who still has power over medicine, regeneration, and healing.

Freyja/Freya: Norse. Called the Mistress of Cats, this goddess was a powerful shapeshifter. She can help with enchantments, good luck, and protection.

Fu-Hsi: China. This god of happiness helps with success.

Fukurokuju: Japan. This is the god of happiness and long life.

Gaea/Gaia: Greece. Known as an Earth goddess, this deity helps with healing.

Ganesha/Ganesh: India. This elephant-headed god is very powerful for removing obstacles.

Hecate: Greece. Known in Thrace as the Triple Goddess of the Moon, she has the power to avert evil and cause transformations.

Hermes: Greece. Known as the Messenger between the gods and humans, this god also rules over orthodox medicine and music.

Hotei Osho: Japan. This rotund little deity is the god of good fortune.

Horus: Egypt. A falcon-headed god, this deity helps with problem solving and success.

Imhotep: Egypt. This is a god of medicine and healing.

Ishtar: Middle East. Called the Queen of Heaven, this goddess helps you overcome obstacles.

Isis: Egypt. This goddess, whose worship lasted long after the collapse of the ancient Egyptian culture, is adept at healing and protection.

Janus: Rome. Originally an Etruscan deity, this god helps with new cycles of life and beginnings and endings.

Kuan Yin: China. This compassionate goddess gives mercy and love.

Lakshmi: India. A goddess of love and creative energy, she is powerful in granting success and good fortune.

Lugh: Ireland, Wales. This famous legendary figure is considered to be a god of healing and magic.

Mukuru: West Africa. This god of rain helps with healing and protection.

Pan: Greece. A god of the woodlands and wild creatures, he is also associated with medicine.

Perun: Russia, Slavonia. Although a god of storms and oracles, he also provides defense against illness.

Sekhmet: Egypt. This fierce lioness-headed goddess is a patroness of physicians and bone-setters.

Shen Nung: China. This deity is a god of medicine.

Shiva: India. Known as the Demon-Slayer, this god is portrayed with four arms. He aids with medicine, healing, and long life.

Tara: India. You can call upon the White Tara for long life and health. The Green Tara is powerful for growth and protection.

Yao-Shih: China. This god is the master of healing.

HEALING ANGELS

Camael: This being helps with courage, purification, and protection.

Gabriel: One of the Archangels, he gives mercy and hope, and helps with herbal medicine.

Michael: One of the Archangels, this being protects and grants guidance in all things.

Raphael: One of the Archangels, he helps with healing, success, and the curing of all diseases.

Tzaphkiel: This angel aids spiritual development, overcoming grief, and helps with the balancing of karma.

HEALING SAINTS

The Infant Jesus of Prague: He aids in health matters, surgery, and guidance.

Our Lady of Guadalupe: Although she helps with any situation, she is powerful in overcoming sickness and bringing peace.

Our Lady of the Immaculate Conception: She helps with all sicknesses.

Our Lady of Lourdes: She helps to heal sicknesses and regain health.

Saint Agnes: She is the patroness of nurses and particularly helpful in curing breast diseases.

Saint Albinus: He aids in curing gallstones and kidney diseases.

Saint Alphonsus Liguori: This saint has power over rheumatic fever, arthritis, osteoarthritis, gout, and joint and muscle ailments.

Saint Bartholomew: He is the patron of surgeons and has power over surgeries.

Saint Cadoc of Wales: He helps with glandular disorders.

Saints Cosmas and Damian: This duo are patrons of druggists, physicians, and surgeons. They also help with getting a correct diagnosis of disease.

Saint Elmo: This saint aids with intestinal diseases.

Saint James the Greater: He helps in removing obstacles, and treating arthritis and rheumatism.

Saint Jude: This saint specializes in helping hopeless cases.

Saint Luke: He is the patron of physicians and surgeons.

Saint Peregrine Laziosi: He helps with health problems, particularly cancer.

Saint Peter: He aids in achieving success, gaining courage and good luck, and removing obstacles.

Saint Philomena: She helps with any desperate situation.

Saint Rita: She aids those in desperate situation and has the power to stop bleeding.

Saint Rita of Cascia: The patroness of hopeless cases, she helps in healing wounds and tumors.

Saint Teresa of Avila: This saint helps with headaches and heart attacks.

The Virgin Mary: Known as the mother of Jesus, this powerful saint will intercede for any need.

You can also add healing stones to your altar, both for their beauty and for their power. Some of the stones you might choose are: moss agate, amazonite, amber, amethyst, aquamarine, beryl, bloodstone, carnelian, chrysocolla, citrine, emerald, fluorite, garnet, hematite, jade, jasper, lapis lazuli, malachite, tourmaline, or turquoise.

Incense will raise the vibrations in any room or house. Examples of healing incenses are: carnation, cedar, cinnamon, gardenia, lavender, lotus, myrrh, orange, rose, and sandalwood. When in doubt, use a blend of frankincense and myrrh, frequently available in stick form. Sticks or cones are fine.

If you choose to burn candles on your altar, you can use either the glass-contained seven-day candles, or six-inch straights in fireproof holders. Seven-day candles usually come in green, blue, or white. These glass-contained candles are meant to be burned steadily for seven days, beginning the day after the new moon. If you can't start a seven-day candle just after the new moon, be certain that you start burning it so it will burn out by the full moon exactly, not a day later. Candles always represent spiritual enlightenment.

The skull candle is another powerful healing candle that some people refuse to use because they don't understand its meaning. Burn one of these for healing serious, deadly, or terminal diseases. It is best burned along with a white candle.

Traditionally, candle colors have specific meanings and uses. A list of these follows.

Black absorbs and removes negatives, protects, release negative energies, and unsticks stagnant situations. It is very powerful, so be careful how you use it.

Light blue is for inspiration, wisdom, protection, good health, happiness, inner peace, and harmony in the home.

Brown influences the earth elementals or energies, balances, and grounds.

Gold or very clear light yellow is used for understanding, fast luck when circumstances are out of your control, healing, and happiness.

Green attracts good fortune, renewal, balance, and healing.

Indigo will aid in balancing out karma.

Magenta is a very high vibrational frequency that makes things happen fast when burned with other colors. It is also useful for quick changes and spiritual healing.

Orange works for adaptability, encouragement, sudden
   changes, success, stamina, and changes luck.
Pink is a gentle color that attracts pure love, spiritual awakening, and healing.
Purple: wisdom, protection, spirit contact, breaking bad luck,
   healing. Use with caution.
Red is more vibrant and is used for energy, courage, will
   power, and good health.
Silver or very clear light gray helps with stability, meditation, removing negative powers, and repelling destructive forces.
White is a color that can be used at any time. It also is for spirituality, wholeness, truth, contacting spirit helpers, and balancing the aura.
Yellow is for power of the mind, confidence, concentration,
   mental clarity, medicine, and healing.

Some cultures add images or pictures of certain animals to
their altars to signify specific energies they wish to attract. If
you want to add animal images, the following list will help you
make a choice.

Bat: good fortune and happiness
Bear: stamina and transformation
Butterfly: reincarnation, transformation, and joy

Cat: healing, seeking hidden information and protection

Cobra: divine wisdom and protection

Coyote: finding opportunities

Deer: contacting spirit guides and gaining intuition

Dog: protection and a willingness to follow through

Dragon: the ability to rise above and conquer obstacles

Dragonfly: seeing the truth and receiving messages of enlightenment

Eagle: wisdom, long life, and connecting with spirit

Elephant: removing obstacles and gaining patience and confidence

Falcon: healing

Hummingbird: happiness

Lion: strength, courage, and releasing stress

Lizard: asking for guidance in difficult situations

Otter: recovering from a crisis

Pegasus or winged horse: changing evil into good

Pig: good health, prosperity, and protection

Tiger: facing an unpleasant situation and dealing with it

Tortoise: long life

Wolf: strength in a fight, wisdom

You can also add any other symbolic object that you connect with healing, willpower, determination, and the spiritual realm. For example, a small table fountain can represent the flow of life force and the receiving of blessings, while keys mean finding a hidden truth or unlocking secrets, perhaps the secret to a cure.

Design your healing altar to represent the sick loved one and your hopes and prayers for healing.

It is my hope that all of the alternative healing techniques in this book will help each healer grow spiritually as well as heal the ones you love. Never give up hope. Never lose your connection with the Divine Source and the greatest healing power in the universe. When you least expect it, your work for healing, however inexperienced you may be, could create a miracle.

Appendix

CHAKRA STONES

Root chakra: Garnet, black obsidian, smoky quartz, hematite, black onyx

Belly chakra: Carnelian, Mexican fire opal

Solar plexus chakra: Golden amber, tiger's eye, citrine, green fluorite, malachite

Heart chakra: Green jade, aventurine, rose quartz, watermelon tourmaline, chrysoprase, malachite

Throat chakra: Azurite, lapis lazuli, chrysocolla, turquoise, blue lace agate

Brow chakra: Sodalite, sugilite, amethyst, purple fluorite, lapis lazuli

Crown chakra: Amethyst, clear quartz; blue, white, or gold fluorite

Transpersonal chakra: Clear quartz crystal

Universal chakra: Rutilated crystal

Hand chakras: Clear quartz crystal, amber, amethyst

Feet chakras: Clear quartz crystal, smoky quartz, black obsidian, black onyx

MAGICAL USES OF COLORS

Black: Absorbs and removes negative vibrations. Breaks up blockages and stagnant situations. Also protects.

Blue: For healing and good health, inner peace, harmony, and spiritual inspiration.

Brown: Good for balance, material needs including money, and concentration.

Gold or clear light yellow: For contacting higher forces, gaining knowledge, and attracting fast luck.

Gray: This neutral color often helps with meditation.

Green: To balance an unstable situation. It also attracts healing energies, good fortune, and success.

Indigo: This dark bluish-purple color is good for meditation, neutralizing negative energies, and clearing out karmic issues.

Magenta: This dark reddish-purple color can be used to bring about quick changes and spiritual healing. It aids all other colors.

Orange: For major sudden changes, encouragement, success, and energy.

Pink: For spiritual awakening, healing, and to banish negativity and depression.

Purple or violet: For psychic ability, spiritual wisdom, progress, contact with spiritual entities, and repelling evil.

Red: For energy, strength, courage, will power, good health, and to repel negative psychic energies.

Silver or clear light gray: Helps neutralize situations and repel destructive forces. It is also good for developing the psychic and meditation.

White: A highly spiritual color, use it for truth, wholeness, balancing the aura, and raising the vibrations in any area. It also attracts spiritual light and mystical knowledge.

PRODUCT SUPPLIERS

For products, first check your local New Age stores. For stones, visit local rock and lapidary shops. Except for candles of certain unusual colors and image candles, you can purchase your candles at discount stores or malls. These candles should be unscented. Herbs and spices in local grocery stores are frequently too old for magical healing use. Instead, check with herb shops, New Age stores, or purchase online from a Pagan supplier.

The following suppliers are ones from whom I frequently make satisfactory purchases and have found to be reliable. Most can be found online. If you prefer a catalog, order one at the online site, write, or call the supplier. Usually these catalogs are free.

Azure Green: www.Azuregreen.com. P.O. Box 48, Middlefield, MA 01243-0048. Phone number: 413-623-2155. Jewelry, stones, oils, incense and burners, herbs, books, bottles and jars, mortars and pestles, herbal teas, music, aromatherapy oils and diffusers, candles including image ones, statues and wall sculptures, bells, talisman bags, divination tools, holy water, and more.

Crescent Moon Goddess: www.crescentmoongoddess.com. Incense and burners, oils, wide variety of candles, aromatherapy oils and diffusers, stones, jewelry, music, divination tools, capes, books, crystals, wands, bath salts, videos, herbs, salves, cauldrons, talisman bags, and more.

Dancing Dragon: www.DancingDragon.com. 5670 West End Rd., No. 4, P.O. Box 1106, Arcata, CA 95518-1106. Phone number: 800-322-6040. Although primarily any object or product with dragons on it, they also have aromatherapy burners and aromatherapy oils.

Edmund Scientific Company: 101 Gloucester Pike, Barrington, NJ 08007. Phone number: 609-573-6250. A wide variety of products, including a large book of colored filters for healing with color.

Nichols Garden Nursery: www.nicholsgardennursery.com. 1190 Old Salem Road, NE, Albany, OR 97321-4580. Phone number: 541-928-9280; toll free for orders 866-408-4851. High-quality herb seeds and plants, herbal teas, oils and soaps, dry potpourri, dry herbs and spices including sweet grass, and gardening books and supplies.

Pacific Spirit, Whole Life Products: 1334 Pacific Avenue, Forest Grove, OR 97116. Phone number: 800-634-9057. Ask for free catalog. Stones and gems, prayer beads, malas, statues, jewelry including copper and magnetic, tonal music, books, prints including angels, videos, and tuning forks.

The Pyramid Collection: www.pyramidcollection.com. Altid Park,

P.O. Box 3333, Chelmsford, MA 01824-0933. Phone number: 800-333-4220. Statues, jewelry, gems and stones, candles, incense and burners, prints, divination tools, books, music, chimes, and talisman bags.

Sacred Source: www.SacredSource.com. P.O. Box 163, Crozet, VA 22932. Phone number: 800-290-6203. Statues of deities and sacred images from around the world, including archangels. Excellent prices.

Tools for Exploration: www.toolsforexploration.com. Email: toolsforexploration@yahoo.com. 9755 Independence Ave., Chatsworth, CA 91311-4318. Phone number: 888-748-6657. A wide array of products, including colored filters and light projectors for color healing. However, this company's products are expensive.

Two Sisters Trading. www.twosisterstrading.com. Phone number: toll free 877-878-9474. Candles, books, jewelry, music, talisman bags, Goddess/Madonna wall pictures, oils, spell kits, angel bowls, divination tools, incense, incense bowls, pocket stones, soaps, and massage oils.

Bibliography

Amber, Reuben. *Color Therapy*. Santa Fe, NM: Aurora Press, 1983.

Anderson, Mary. *Colour Healing*. UK: Aquarian Press, 1981.

Ashley-Farrand, Thomas. *Healing Mantras*. (Compact disc) Boulder, CO: Sounds True, 1999.

_____. *Healing Mantras*. (Book). NY: Ballantine Wellspring, 1999.

_____. *The Power of Mantras*. (Compact disc) Boulder, CO: Sounds True, 1999.

Bernstein, Albert J. *Emotional Vampires: Dealing With People Who Drain You Dry*. NY: McGraw-Hill Companies, 2000.

Beyerl, Paul. *The Master Book of Herbalism*. Custer, WA: Phoenix Publishing, 1984.

Bhattacharya, A. K. *Gem Therapy*. Calcutta, India: Firma KLM Private Ltd., 1992.

Bibb, Benjamin O. and Joseph J. Weed. *Amazing Secrets of Psychic Healing*. West Nyack, NY: Parker Publishing, 1976.

Brennan, Barbara Ann. *Hands of Light: A Guide to Healing Through the Human Energy Field*. NY: Bantam Books, 1988.

Brier, Bob. *Ancient Egyptian Magic*. NY: Quill, 1981.

Bruyere, Rosalyn L. Editor, Jeanne Farrens. *Wheels of Light: A Study of the Chakras*. Arcadia, CA: Bon Productions, 1989.

Bryan, Cyril P., translator. *Ancient Egyptian Medicine: The Papyrus Ebers*. Chicago, IL: Ares Publishers, 1974.

Bryant, Ina. *Magnetic Electricity a Life Saver*. Kingsport, TN: Kingsport Press, 1978.

Budge, E. A. Wallis. *Amulets & Superstitions*. NY: Dover Publications, 1978.

_____. *The Divine Origin of the Craft of the Herbalist*. NY: Dover Publications, 1996. Originally published 1928.

_____. *Egyptian Magic*. NY: Dover Publications, 1971.

_____. *Gods of the Egyptians*. 2 volumes. NY: Dover Publications, 1969.

Budilovsky, Joan and Eve Adamson. *The Complete Idiot's Guide to Meditation*. NY: Alpha Books, 1999.

Campbell, Don. *The Mozart Effect*. NY: Avon Books, 1997.

Chadwick, Gloria. *Discovering Your Past Lives*. Chicago, IL: Contemporary Books, 1988.

Chopra, Deepak. *Creating Health*. Boston, MA: Houghton Mifflin Co., 1987.

Conway, D. J. *The Ancient & Shining Ones*. St. Paul, MN: Llewellyn Publications, 1993.

_____. *Laying on of Stones*. Freedom, CA: The Crossing Press, 1999.

_____. *A Little Book of Altar Magic*. Freedom, CA: The Crossing Press, 2000.

_____. *A Little Book of Candle Magic*. Freedom, CA: The Crossing Press, 2000.

_____. *A Little Book of Pendulum Magic*. Freedom, CA: The Crossing Press, 2001.

_____. *Wicca: The Complete Craft*. Freedom, CA: The Crossing Press, 2001.

Cunningham, Scott. *Cunningham's Encyclopedia of Magical Herbs*. St. Paul, MN: Llewellyn Publications, 1985.

Davidson, Gustav. *Dictionary of Angels*. NY: The Free Press, 1967.

Dossey, Larry. *Healing Words: The Power of Prayer and the Practice of Medicine*. NY: HarperCollins, 1993.

Eden, Donna. *Energy Medicine*. NY: Jeremy P. Tarcher, 1998.

Farmer, David. *The Oxford Dictionary of Saints*. UK: Oxford University Press, 1997.

Gardner, Joy. *Color and Crystals*. Freedom, CA: The Crossing Press, 1988.

Gawain, Shakti. *Creative Visualization*. NY: Bantam Books, 1982.

Gaynor, Mitchell L. *Sounds of Healing*. NY: Broadway Books, 1999.

Georgian, Linda. *Your Guardian Angel*. NY: Simon & Schuster, 1994.

Gerber, Richard. *Vibrational Medicine for the 21st Century*. NY: Eagle Brook, 2000.

Goldman, Jonathan. *Healing Sounds: The Power of Harmonics*. UK: Element Books, 1999.

Gonzalez-Wippler, Migene. *The Complete Book of Amulets & Talismans*. St. Paul, MN: Llewellyn Publications, 1991.

Hall, Manley P. *The Secret Teachings of All Ages*. Los Angeles, CA: Philosophical Research Society, 1977.

Hay, Louise. *You Can Heal Your Life*. Carlsbad, CA: Hay House, 1999.

Hirshberg, Caryle and Marc Ian Barasch. *Remarkable Recovery*. NY: Riverhead Press, 1995.

Howard, Michael. *Finding Your Guardian Angel*. UK: Thorsons, 1991.

_____. *The Runes & Other Magical Alphabets*. UK: Aquarian Press, 1981.

Howes, Michael. *Amulets*. NY: St. Martin's Press, 1975.

Hunt, Valerie. *Infinite Mind: The Science of Human Vibrations*. Malibu, CA: Malibu, 1995.

Judith, Anodea. *Wheels of Life: A User's Guide to the Chakra System*. St. Paul, MN: Llewellyn Publications, 1993.

Kamal, Hassan. *Dictionary of Pharaonic Medicine*. Cairo, Egypt: The National Publication House, 1967.

Karagulla, Shafica and Dora van Gelder Kunz. *The Chakras and the Human Energy Fields*. Wheaton, IL: Quest Books, 1989.

Khalsa, Dharma Singh and Cameron Stauth. *Meditation as Medicine*. NY: Pocket Books, 2001.

Kilner, W. J. *The Aura*. York Beach, ME: Samuel Weiser, 1984.

Klotsche, Charles. *Color Medicine*. Sedona, AZ: Light Technology Publishing.

Kriegger, Delores. *The Therapeutic Touch*. NJ: Prentice-Hall, 1979.

Krystal, Phyllis. *Cutting the Ties That Bind*. Los Angeles, CA: Aura Books, 1982.

Leadbeater, C. W. *The Chakras*. Wheaton, IL: The Theosophical Publishing House, 1927.

Lewis, James R. and Evelyn Dorothy Oliver. *Angels A to Z*. NY: Visible Ink, 1996.

Lippman, Deborah and Paul Colin. *How to Make Amulets, Charms, and Talismans*. NY: E. Evans & Co., 1974.

Malbrough, Ray T. *The Magical Power of the Saints*. St. Paul, MN: Llewellyn Publications, 1998.

McManus, Jason, editor. *Powers of Healing*. Alexandria, VA: Time-Life, 1989.

Meadows, Kenneth. *Rune Power*. Boston, MA: Element Books, 1996.

Mesko, Sabrina. *Healing Mudras: Yoga for Your Hands*. NY: Ballantine Wellspring, 2000.

Morris, Desmond. *Body Guards*. UK: Element Books, 1999.

Motoyama, Hiroshi and R. Brown. *Science and the Evolution of Consciousness: Chakras, Ki, and Psi*. Brookline, MA: Autumn Press, 1978.

Myss, Caroline. *Why People Don't Heal and How They Can*. NY: Three Rivers Press, 1997.

Ostrander, Sheila and Lynn Schroeder. *Psychic Discoveries Behind the Iron Curtain*. NJ: Prentice-Hall, 1970.

Ouseley, S. G. J. *The Power of the Rays: The Science of Colour-Healing*. UK: L. N. Fowler & Co., 1976.

_____. *The Science of the Aura*. UK: L. N. Fowler & Co., 1973.

Pennick, Nigel. *The Complete Illustrated Guide to Runes*. UK: Element Books, 1999.

_____. *Magical Alphabets*. York Beach, ME: Samuel Weiser, 1992.

Petrie, William Flinders. *Amulets*. UK: Aris & Phillips, Ltd., 1972.

Quirke, Stephen. *Ancient Egyptian Religion*. NY: Dover Publications, 1992.

Regardie, Israel. *How to Make and Use Talismans*. UK: Aquarian Press, 1981.

Rosetree, Rose. *Aura Reading Through All Your Senses*. Sterling, VA: Women's Intuition Worldwide, 1996.

Sandoval, Annette. *The Directory of Saints: A Concise Guide to Patron Saints*. NY: Signet/Penguin, 1997.

Schulz, Mona Lisa. *Awakening Intuition*. NY: Three Rivers Press, 1998.

Sher, Barbara. *Wishcraft: How to Get What You Really Want*. NY: Ballantine Books, 1979.

Skelton, Robin. *Talismanic Magic*. York Beach, ME: Samuel Weiser, 1985.

Smith, Michael G. *Crystal Power*. St. Paul, MN: Llewellyn Publications, 1985.

_____. *Crystal Spirit*. St. Paul, MN: Llewellyn Publications, 1990.

_____, and Lin Westhorp. *Crystal Warrior: Shamanic Transformation and Projection of Universal Energy*. St. Paul, MN: Llewellyn Publications, 1993.

Snellgrove, Brian. *The Magic in Your Hands*. UK: The C. W. Daniel Company, 1997.

Thomas, William and Kate Pavitt. *The Book of Talismans, Amulets, & Zodiacal Gems*. North Hollywood, CA: Wilshire Book Co., 1970.

Thompson, C. J. S. *Celtic Healing: The Healing Arts of Ancient Britain, Wales and Ireland*. Edmonds, WA: Sure Fire Press, 1994.

Walker, Barbara G. *The Woman's Dictionary of Symbols & Sacred Objects*. San Francisco, CA: Harper & Row, 1988.

Walker, Morton. *The Power of Color*. Garden City, NY: Avery Publishing, 1989.

Webb, Marcus & Maria. *Healing Touch*. NY: Sterling Publishing, 1999.

Weinman, Ric A. *Your Hands Can Heal: Learn to Channel Healing Energy*. NY: E. P. Dutton, 1988.